PRAISE FOR *REST & WAR*

"We've all felt battle-weary and discouraged at times in our lives as Christians. Ben Stuart knows what this feels like and teaches readers to know the right time to rest and the right time to war, with Jesus by our side. In *Rest & War*, you'll find the companion you've been waiting for as you look to honor God with the way you spend your days and mental energy. Life may not always be easy, but this book will help you learn to live your one life well!"

LYSA TERKEURST, BESTSELLING AUTHOR AND
PRESIDENT OF PROVERBS 31 MINISTRIES

"Profound yet practical. Ben has made a habit of examining Scripture to mine the truth from the text, and this book is proof of that pursuit. In *Rest & War*, he's stepped into a cultural crisis and held up a beacon of light and hope through the person and way of Jesus. From the earliest chapters in Genesis, we see our God creating structure in a way that brings about life and flourishing, and that is what Ben is offering in this book: strategic structure that doesn't just change your schedule but changes your heart as well."

LOUIE GIGLIO, BESTSELLING AUTHOR, PASTOR OF PASSION
CITY CHURCH, AND FOUNDER OF PASSION CONFERENCES

"There is a war for our faith, and *Rest & War* will give you the tools and courage to fight."

JENNIE ALLEN, BESTSELLING AUTHOR AND
FOUNDER OF IF:GATHERING

"*Rest & War* is a breath of fresh air for our generation. Ben's practical and encouraging words help us all learn how to better cultivate true intimacy with Jesus as we navigate the complexities of our daily lives."

SADIE ROBERTSON HUFF, BESTSELLING AUTHOR,
SPEAKER, AND FOUNDER OF LIVE ORIGINAL

"One of the most common answers I hear when I ask someone 'How are you?' is, 'I'm tired.' It reveals how the pace of our world is often at war with the steadfast way of living Jesus invites us to. *Rest & War* is a book that intentionally examines and practically equips you to live out the rhythms of Jesus in our modern-day world."

KYLE IDLEMAN, BESTSELLING AUTHOR AND PASTOR OF LOUISVILLE'S SOUTHEAST CHRISTIAN CHURCH

"*Rest & War* offers the ingredients needed not just to face the chaos of life, but to come out stronger on the other side. Ben clearly communicates the ways to struggle well in a world that does not know rest. This resource will help you navigate this beautiful tension in your spiritual life and set in place disciplines that will help you flourish."

LEVI LUSKO, BESTSELLING AUTHOR AND PASTOR OF FRESH LIFE CHURCH

"Ben Stuart is a needed voice in the chaotic world we face today! I am so thankful he has put pen to paper in order to help us navigate the spiritual life and flourish. Life is hard, but God is good. Thank you, Ben, for this resource!"

CROWDER, CHRISTIAN MUSIC SINGER, SONGWRITER, AND THREE-TIME GRAMMY NOMINEE

"*Rest & War* is a game-changing, difference-making, paradigm-shifting book. It's a guide and encouragement to live out the fullness of faith and to deflect the deception of empty lies. Ben masterfully weaves wit and wisdom to set a clear path for our journey. Read this book with your heart and put it to action in your steps as you fulfill God's purpose for your life."

GREGG MATTE, AUTHOR AND PASTOR OF HOUSTON'S FIRST BAPTIST CHURCH

"I truly believe that Ben Stuart is one of the most effective communicators of God's Word in this generation. Whether the word is preached, written, or spoken in a conversation, I always walk away saying, "I get it!" In *Rest & War*, Ben gives us a simple, sound, and strategic game plan on finding our rest in the Lord while engaging in life's unrelenting battles. Thank you, brother. *God's . . . perfect . . . timing!*"

MIKADO HINSON, DIRECTOR OF FOOTBALL PLAYER DEVELOPMENT FOR TEXAS A&M

WE GO TO WAR THAT WE MAY HAVE PEACE.

—AUGUSTINE

REST
&
WAR.

RHYTHMS OF A WELL-FOUGHT LIFE

REST & WAR

BEN STUART

W Publishing Group

An Imprint of Thomas Nelson

passionpublishing

Published in Nashville, Tennessee, by W Publishing, an imprint of Thomas Nelson.

Thomas Nelson titles may be purchased in bulk for educational, business, fundraising, or sales promotional use. For information, please email SpecialMarkets@ThomasNelson.com.

Unless otherwise noted, Scripture quotations are taken from the ESV® Bible (The Holy Bible, English Standard Version®). Copyright © 2001 by Crossway, a publishing ministry of Good News Publishers. Used by permission. All rights reserved.

Scripture quotations marked NASB are taken from the New American Standard Bible® (NASB). Copyright © 1960, 1971, 1977, 1995, 2020 by The Lockman Foundation. Used by permission. www.lockman.org

Scripture quotations marked NIV are taken from The Holy Bible, New International Version®, NIV®. Copyright © 1973, 1978, 1984, 2011 by Biblica, Inc.® Used by permission of Zondervan. All rights reserved worldwide. www.Zondervan.com. The "NIV" and "New International Version" are trademarks registered in the United States Patent and Trademark Office by Biblica, Inc.®

Scripture quotations marked NKJV are taken from the New King James Version®. Copyright © 1982 by Thomas Nelson. Used by permission. All rights reserved.

Scripture quotations marked NLT are taken from the Holy Bible, New Living Translation. Copyright © 1996, 2004, 2015 by Tyndale House Foundation. Used by permission of Tyndale House Publishers, Inc., Carol Stream, Illinois 60188. All rights reserved.

All italicized words in Scripture quotations designate the author's emphasis.

Any internet addresses, phone numbers, or company or product information printed in this book are offered as a resource and are not intended in any way to be or to imply an endorsement by Thomas Nelson, nor does Thomas Nelson vouch for the existence, content, or services of these sites, phone numbers, companies, or products beyond the life of this book.

ISBN 978-0-7852-4833-0 (audiobook)
ISBN 978-0-7852-4832-3 (eBook)
ISBN 978-0-7852-4831-6 (TP)

Library of Congress Control Number: 2021945778

Printed in the United States of America

22 23 24 25 26 LSC 10 9 8 7 6 5 4 3 2 1

To Hannah, Sparrow, and Owen
Your daddy delights in you.

CONTENTS

CONTENTS

PART 1

A STRUGGLE,
A SAVIOR,
AND A STRATEGY

CHAPTER 1

THE SURVIVAL GUIDE

Oh God, we are so stupid.

These were the first words of my friend Ben's prayer. I don't remember his next few lines. I wasn't really paying attention. My eyes kept scanning the snow-covered mountains under our perch high atop Longs Peak. As we sat there near the highest point in Rocky Mountain National Park, entirely depleted physically, I wondered, *How long until our friends down below file a missing person's report? Can a rescue helicopter reach this altitude?* The only thing I knew for certain was that I could not conceive of a way to get down that mountain using only my internal resources. How did I let myself end up here?

It had started out so well. I had joined a team of college students from around the country in a summer-long internship with a ministry in Denver, Colorado. Early in our trip my new friend, Ben, asked if I wanted to climb this massive fourteen-thousand-foot mountain with him. I said sure, and we immediately began to train. We resolved to summit Longs Peak one month later.

When the day arrived, our ascent began well. We bounded up the trail, passing lesser hikers, making great time. We leapt through the boulder field and arrived ahead of schedule at the critical transition point, known as the Keyhole. The name came from the rock formation's shape—erosion had created a rock archway that, from a distance, resembled a keyhole. But this alone did not account for the title.

This waypoint on the trail also represented a critical juncture in the journey, when the path began winding around the back side of the mountain, a part previously not visible from the trail. The trail narrowed to a sliver of a path a few feet above a precipitous cliff. One false move there, and you'd disappear over a blind edge, careening into a distant valley below.

On the day Ben and I were hiking, the Keyhole marked another critical change in our journey: the presence of snow. Fortunately for us, a mountaineer had been there before us. We could see a set of footprints in the deep snow and singular holes in the snowbank on the high side of the mountain, where no doubt a hiking stick had been used. We carefully placed our feet in the footprints and our fingers in the holes as we picked our way across the ledge.

After a few perilous yards along the cliff's edge, the path turned steeply upward, ascending up the snow-covered mountainside. The footprints continued, and we turned to climb them like a ladder, hugging the side of the mountain.

At this moment something suddenly began to shift for Ben and me. My internal energy gauge began to plummet. My lungs struggled for air, and my limbs, in addition to being wet and cold from the snow, began to feel heavy. Each heave of my body upward required an enormous expenditure of energy. At the midway point I glanced up at Ben and watched his head collapse with exhaustion into the snow. He was feeling it too. But this was not the moment to stop! We heaved ourselves up several feet, finally reaching the thin, rocky path above.

From there, we followed the marked route around a corner, only to find another corner ahead. And another. And another. After what felt like an eternity, we rounded yet another corner—and saw before us a steep incline through the snow. At the sight of it, Ben dropped down to the ground. I halfheartedly tried to spur him on but then crumpled down next to him on the trail. We were exhausted. Depleted. Nauseous. And stuck. After a few moments of listening to the wind whistle through the mountain range below, our prayer acknowledging our stupidity began.

Then it happened. For a split second, while Ben was praying and I was looking around in desperation, I saw a human head pop out from behind a boulder. It was so fast, I wondered if I'd imagined it. *Am I hallucinating? Has it gotten that bad?* Our prayer ended. We sat in silence and watched the world from above. And then, from behind another boulder, the head arrived! Attached to a person!

The mountain man made his way over to us and struck up a conversation. "Hey, guys!" he shouted, his high-volume positivity a stark contrast to our complete despair.

We grunted a response.

Undaunted by our lack of enthusiasm, he continued, "Great day to hike! You guys been to the top yet?" Then, without waiting for an answer, he surveyed us briefly and remarked, "Wait a second, you're the college guys who came up here without equipment. We heard about you! We are in awe of you guys. You're crazy!" He then returned to his original question: "You been to the top?"

I responded by telling him we had not and were not planning to. He found this to be unbelievable.

"You have to go. C'mon guys!" At this point I could tell that his relentlessly upbeat attitude was starting to grate on Ben, so I stood up on my wobbly legs and sidebarred our conversation. I whispered to him, "We are not doing well—we are totally exhausted. There is no way we can go any farther."

My admission of our frailty changed his demeanor. I remember him staring down at my hands. I had them wrapped in my soaking wet sleeves, trying to get them warm.

"Wait a minute," he replied, then set down his pack and produced two pairs of mittens—well, mittens is really not quite the right word. They were coverings for your hands, but they extended up to the elbow and had multiple straps that could bind them tightly to your forearm. "Put these on," he said, handing them to us.

Ben and I eagerly put on the mittens and felt exquisite relief as warmth returned to our fingers.

The mountain man continued to parent us. "First things first, gentlemen. You are breathing wrong."

This surprised us. Of all our problems on the mountain, knowing how to breathe did not seem to be one of them. I'd always considered breathing to be an involuntary action that did not require conscious management.

He noted our looks of skepticism that implied, *I think we know how to breathe, man.* I will never forget his next words. He told us, "You are in a new environment. The atmosphere has changed. You have to adapt if you want to survive."

THE ATMOSPHERE HAS CHANGED

I think about that moment often as I survey the cultural landscape of our world today. Shifts in the atmosphere of society have had a profound impact on our vibrancy and the way we interact with God, one another, and even ourselves. Because these changes are simply in the atmosphere, we can't always see them. But we can *feel* them. And recent data backs this up: there is something about modern life that does not promote human flourishing.

Anxiety and depression, particularly among young people in the United States, have been consistently on the rise since 2008.[1] Recent data collected for a joint study by the US Census Bureau and the Centers for Disease Control and Prevention indicate this: "During August 2020–February 2021, the percentage of adults with recent symptoms of an anxiety or a depressive disorder increased from 36.4% to 41.5%. . . . Increases were largest among adults aged 18–29 years."[2]

The increased political and philosophical polarization in our society incites fear, uncertainty, and anger. The constant comparison of our lives with others' pristine presentations on social media fills many with discouragement. And the irresistible lure of our screens means we are constantly soaking our minds in this polarization and comparison, which feed our stress and despair.

In the atmosphere of anxiety, the traditional buffers from stress have been removed. One professor of psychology at San Diego State University reported that from 2000 to 2015 the number of high school students who got together daily with their friends dropped by 40 percent.[3]

Cigna, a global health services company, reported that loneliness has "reached epidemic proportions in the United States, as people of all ages and backgrounds struggle to find a sense of belonging."[4] Among their findings: only half of Americans say they have meaningful in-person interactions on a daily basis.

In the atmosphere of relentless restlessness and shallow social connections, addiction has risen to new heights. Alcohol, drugs, pornography, and incessant scrolling on our screens have all become habits to distract us from stress. However, rather than alleviating our problems, they've created more problems and have only increased the anxiety and isolation we've attempted to escape. When you think about all of that, it's hardly surprising that in 2019 Gallup recorded the lowest levels of happiness in the United States in their seventy-plus years of researching well-being.[5]

We aren't looking so good.

In the relatively safest time for human beings to exist on the planet, we find ourselves disoriented and disturbed. Like Ben and me on that mountainside, we are exhausted, discouraged, and uncertain about how to address our situation. We need to realize that the atmosphere has changed, and we must adapt if we want to survive.

What's the answer? What do we do next?

THE PATH TOWARD REST FOR THE SOUL

We need a guide to emerge upon the mountain who will equip us, teach us, and show us how to move forward.

Centuries ago the prophet Jeremiah looked out upon a generation that felt unsure of where to turn in the midst of crisis and uncertainty. He declared,

> Thus says the Lord:
> "Stand by the roads, and look,
> 	and ask for the ancient paths,
> where the good way is; and walk in it,
> 	and find rest for your souls." (Jeremiah 6:16)

Many are standing at a critical crossroads, asking where the good way is. In this book I want to show you the ancient path that leads to rest for our souls.

I started my ministry career with an unbounded zeal and optimism. I was going to use my gifts to do great things for God! But within the first five years, I watched five men I knew personally drop out of ministry because of moral failures. Then over the next few years, I watched men I had patterned my life after take extended leaves of absence because of emotional burnout, discouragement, or depression. My goal had been to succeed, but I began to realize that a big part of success was figuring out how to *survive*.

As I crossed from my twenties into my thirties, I appeared to have everything together. I had a great marriage. I was leading a large and vibrant ministry on the campus of a major university. I had a steady income, career success, and strong relationships. I was charging up the mountain of life! All this was true. But it was also true that wounds from my parents' divorce, struggles from my past, and my personal insecurities were along for the ride. And the higher I ascended in ministry, the more depleted I felt. External setbacks, discouragements, whispers of comparison, and technological shifts exposed many of my internal weaknesses. The atmosphere had shifted, and I lacked the internal resources to keep moving forward.

So for the past twenty years of my life, I have passionately sought out strategies for surviving and thriving, not only in ministry but in life. To be sure, I've needed encouragement, but more than inspiration, I've needed information. What were the survival skills that would keep me fueled and moving forward?

In the searching, I discovered what many before me have as well: admitting you need help is the first step toward victory. Humility is the doorway to wisdom. As I listened to the voices of mentors, teachers, friends, and, perhaps most of all, the theologian John Owen, I began to assemble for myself a compendium of the strategies and structures of the spiritual life. Now, I want to share them with you.

YOUR PERSONAL GUIDE
FOR THE JOURNEY

When Jesus looked at the crowds in his day, he saw women and men who were "harassed and helpless, like sheep without a shepherd" (Matthew 9:36). They were relentlessly bombarded with trouble and lacked the resources to defend themselves. But Jesus did not shake his head or wag a finger at them and scold them. Rather, "he had compassion for them" and taught them many things (v. 36).

Most of us feel distraught by the constant uncertainty and anxiety surrounding us and by the fear, lust, pride, and doubt within us. Often, we don't know how to manage any of it. We feel helpless.

The good news is, we have a Guide. He looks at us not with eyes of condemnation but with eyes of compassion. And he has many things to teach us if we have ears to listen.

What you will find in the pages ahead is not a scolding for your struggles, nor is it an extended motivational speech to try harder. I want to bring you to the Good Shepherd, who can lead us in a day of trouble. I want to show you the ancient path that leads to rest for our souls. I want to equip you to adapt and advance toward your God-given destiny.

Think of this book more as a field guide than a motivational seminar. When you are hiking through the unknown, yes, you need some inspiration, but what you need even more is good information.

High atop that snow-covered peak, our guide showed us the

rhythms of how to pause and rest, then push to advance. Granted, we had been taking breaks on our way up the mountain, then pushing hard to climb. But we were inefficient. Unskilled. And our exhaustion reflected that.

Our hero taught us how to take productive rest by focusing on our breathing and refueling with water and food, and then attack the next challenge before us with intense purpose. There was a rhythm to it. Pause, then pursue. Rest, then war.

THE STRUGGLE IS REAL

God wants to equip us to ascend to heights we cannot reach on our own. However, we must realize that there are no shortcuts to a truly spiritual life, no life hacks to avoid the hard parts. There is real struggle involved. There also can be real gains—real ground covered and strength built. But to experience serenity, we must struggle. To find peace, we must train our hands for war.

I imagine that if you picked up a book like this it is because you desire some kind of peace with God. You know that your life is meant for more than just accumulating experiences and accoutrements. You want to know God and be a part of what he is doing in the world. You want to tap into your full potential and use it for the best of all purposes. You want to *live*. Unencumbered. Undistracted. With mental clarity and heartfelt passion.

Yet you do not have to live long in this world before you realize that the pursuit of intimacy with God is not easy. It is hard. It's a fight! A life of spirituality is lived in the context of adversity.

When we try to read the Scriptures, all manner of competing thoughts and rival affections come raging forward. If we do manage to learn something, worries, fears, and distractions can rise up and choke out these God-given insights before they can produce any real fruit in our lives (Luke 8:4–8). Often we feel as though we live in Romans 7:15: "I do not understand my own actions. . . . I do not do what I want, but I do the very thing I hate."

Many of us honestly do not feel a hunger for God or sense of purpose in life; those feelings are muted by the static of low-grade guilt over our besetting struggles, always humming in the background of our entire story. The wet blanket of constant failure dampens the fire of our affection for the Lord and passion for living.

Some of you reading this find yourself deeply discouraged. You are plagued by desires, impulses, addictions that you want to be free from. You have asked God many times to take them away, and he hasn't. So maybe you try to rationalize that what you are doing is okay and make some kind of uneasy peace with it. But the guilt remains. You are asking, *Is this just who I am? Is this the best it can be?*

Others of you have come to terms with the fact that life comes with headwinds. You've read the New Testament and seen words like *battle, war, conflict,* and *struggle* peppered throughout the text, describing the life of a Christian. You understand that in this life we will have trouble (John 16:33). You want a guide and a strategy because the methods you have employed so far are not working.

For much of my life, spirituality was built around the camp-high experience. My friends and I would show up at our weeklong summer camp completely dominated by the powerful forces of our insecurities, lusts, and pride. For three to four days we would live crazy. But by the last night of camp, everybody got saved. Exhaustion coupled with malnourishment from eating cafeteria food left us in an emotionally volatile state. Then a protracted worship service would leave us all emotionally worked up. By the end we would all be crying, singing "friends are friends forever," and stepping up to the microphone to make big promises about what we'd do for God. Within a week we all would break every promise we'd made and sit alone in our rooms, surrounded by the same old addictions, asking ourselves, *What's wrong with me?*

I have met many Christians who have spent years on the "spiritual-high roller coaster" and ultimately have seen very little progress. If that is you, then you are in the right place. I am here to acknowledge that we often feel like we are in a war because we *are!* The pursuit of intimacy with God occurs in the context of adversity.

Together we're going to embrace the fact that life is a struggle, better understand our situation with all its attendant difficulties, and zero in on a strategy to struggle *well.*

KNOW THE ONE WHO'S
FOUGHT FOR YOU

Before Ben and I could receive guidance, we needed to meet our guide and get to know him. The same is true for us as we pursue growth. Before we try to improve our lives, we need to meet the Author of life. Before we attempt to implement guidance, we need to meet the Guide. And it is actually even bigger than that. Before we attempt to fight, we need to know the One who first fought for us.

Indeed, the best fighters are those who know that they have been fought for.

We see this in children. Studies reveal that kids raised in two-parent homes perform better at every measurable test than kids without that support.[6] This doesn't mean you are doomed if you did not have that; God accomplishes eternal impact with broken instruments. But

THE BEST FIGHTERS ARE THOSE WHO KNOW THAT THEY HAVE BEEN FOUGHT FOR.

RHYTHMS OF A WELL-FOUGHT LIFE

REST & WAR

AUTHORED BY BEN STUART

we do well to analyze that truth. Young people who did not witness an adult fight for them, choose them, or endure hardship for them are more likely to quit on themselves. We need someone to choose us. Prefer us. Sacrifice for us. Fight for us. When we see this happen, it not only fills our hearts with love, it invites us to do the same—to enter the same battle of choosing, fighting for, and sacrificing our lives for something greater.

When Goliath shouted his threats at the Israelite armies, they cowered in fear. But when David defeated Goliath in the valley, the Israelites found the confidence to run forward and drive the Philistines out of their land. Before we can drive out the little Philistines that plague us, we must first understand the war we are part of, the one the Son of David, Jesus, has fought in.

I want to call you to battle and to build. I'm not talking about fighting little skirmishes in life for your ego or building flimsy kingdoms that will fall like a house of cards. I want you to expend your maximum energy for the greatest of all causes. I want you to fight the battle of the ages and build a kingdom that will never fade. But in order to do this, you must first understand that the King of kings has fought for you.

CHAPTER 2

THE CONQUERING KING

Years ago a small group of my friends got together to watch a video from our Navy SEAL buddy's latest training: HALO jumping. The acronym HALO stands for "high altitude, low opening." It's a parachuting technique that multiple branches of the military are trained to use, and it is *intense*! The trainees spend one day attending briefings in a classroom. By day two they are leaping out of airplanes flying more than four miles above the earth.

The training video consisted of helmet-cam shots the instructors took as they trained the men in the air. At the outset it was obvious these coaches were having a little fun at their students' expense when they created this video. As the first terrified-looking student arrived at the door of the aircraft, the video editor had added some kind of circus music. This poor young man, as soon as he hit the air, remained upright and began to feverishly pump his arms and legs. It looked like he was trying to run in place. We were screaming at the TV, "There's no traction up there, brother! Lean!" Other trainees fared better, but the video kept a tone of silliness.

Yet with each successive jump, they gained a new skill. They mastered the technique of turning their bodies at exact degrees. They learned how to drop their arms and tack through the air at speeds of over one hundred miles an hour. With each descent they began to look less and less funny and more and more impressive.

As the video neared its conclusion, I noticed none of us were laughing anymore. We watched in silence as these soldiers loaded themselves into the plane one last time. They had sixty pounds of gear strapped to their bodies, including multiple weapons. When the time came to approach the door of the aircraft, they did not look nervous. When the signal was given, they leapt from the plane without hesitation. As they descended they controlled their bodies with exact movements.

It dawned on me why the mood had shifted in the room as we watched. We had all just been reminded what these training exercises were all about. These guys were not just a group of buddies taking skydiving lessons for fun. They were fighters preparing to be inserted behind enemy lines. They'd be ready to jump at high altitudes so the enemy would not hear the plane. They'd open their parachutes low so they could spend the least amount of time in the air as an open target. This wasn't a joyride. They were warriors with a mission to rescue people in danger and wreak havoc on those who'd oppressed them.

As I watched the final man descend through the night sky I thought, *Now that is just like Jesus.*

Listen to what 1 John 3:8 tells us: "The Son of God appeared for this purpose, to destroy the works of the devil" (NASB). Jesus came to destroy something.

You may object, "Wait. I thought he came to save, to bring peace, to heal. What do you mean *destroy?*"

Think about it:

To save means there was a person or force holding people captive that must be overcome.

To bring peace suggests a prior state where there was no peace.

To heal suggests there was a disease or a sickness that must be cut out.

For Jesus to save, bring peace, and heal, he had to destroy something. *Liberation required destruction.*

WHAT DID JESUS COME
TO DESTROY?

John told us Jesus came to destroy "the works of the devil." Now, I realize that some may say, "The *devil*? Really? Red jumpsuit, tail, little pointy horns? Isn't that a bit of an arcane notion? I have a hard time believing all that."

C. S. Lewis, the beloved author who converted from atheism to Christianity in his thirties, said, "One of the things that surprised me when I first read the New Testament seriously was that it talked so much about a Dark Power in the universe—a mighty evil spirit who was held to be the Power behind death and disease, and sin. . . . Christianity agrees . . . that this universe is at war."[1]

If you find it difficult to take seriously the idea of a spiritual struggle in the background of our lives, then consider this: if you do not believe it, then you must produce a philosophy that explains how a creation as beautiful as humanity can inflict upon itself so much horror.

How do you account for the hundreds of millions killed by their own governments in the twentieth century? How do you explain the atrocities that appear in the news every day, or the vile way we speak to one another online? How do you explain the evil lurking in our hearts, our violation of our own personal standards of morality, and our callous indifference to global suffering? The selfishness we see running rampant in our own experience, the pain in our own story, the apathy in our own hearts—it transcends ethnicity, culture, time, and education. It is a human condition. And the Scriptures declare that it is orchestrated. We most certainly have an Enemy working against us.

The Scriptures refer to him as the devil, which simply means "accuser." In Hebrew he is called Satan, a word that means "opponent" or "adversary." Jesus called him the "ruler of this world" (John 12:31). Paul called him "the god of this age" and "the spirit that is now at work in the sons of disobedience" (2 Corinthians 4:4 NIV; Ephesians 2:2). John ominously said, "We know that we are from God, and the whole world lies in the power of the evil one" (1 John 5:19).

Behind it all is a consciousness. And he is waging a war.

THE WORK OF THE ENEMY

John said, "The one who practices sin is of the devil; for the devil has been sinning from the beginning" (1 John 3:8 NASB).

The word "sin" carries the idea of a violation of a standard. There was a mark we were meant to hit, and we didn't hit it. As human beings there was something great we were meant to be, and we have fallen short of it. The Scriptures affirm what we often feel: we are not what we are meant to be.

Earlier in the passage John explained, "Everyone who practices sin also practices lawlessness; and sin is lawlessness" (1 John 3:4 NASB). This does not suggest that God is like a heavenly Santa checking his list to see if you have been naughty or nice. It is more comprehensive than that.

God's law is his revealed will for his creation. He created all things to work together in mutually beneficial harmony. He created physical laws that govern the universe. We see the earth orbiting around the sun, spinning on its axis, giving us seasons, days, and years, and it all makes sense. In the book of Proverbs we are told that "by wisdom" the earth was made (3:19). There is a logic to how it all fits together.

Proverbs also says of wisdom that "all her paths are peace" (3:17). The word we translate "peace" is the Hebrew word *shalom*. This word means much more than the absence of conflict; it also means the presence of flourishing. When all things work as God designed, then all things benefit. Rain falls and waters the earth. That earth brings forth crops. These feed us, and we in turn care for the soil. Everyone wins.[2]

These governing laws of God also apply to relationships. Men were meant to love and value women as coheirs in the grace of life. Women were made to respect and encourage men. Parents were designed to care for their children and help develop the gifts God placed in them. Communities were designed to foster human flourishing at every level as people work together for the common good. Words were meant to be used to speak to one another in kindness. All creation worships God and he satisfies all. This is shalom, the way it should be, the way God created the world to run.

But the adversary came to disrupt it all. And John said he's been doing it since the beginning.

He convinced our first parents that in order to really enjoy life they had to rebel against the Author of life. Today he tries to convince us that if we truly want the best life has to offer we must go our own way; we must determine what is right or wrong. The lawlessness he sells us is that our ideas are better than God's.

When our first parents believed this, devastation ensued.

They got the experience they wanted. But they got something they did not expect: shame. Immediately after they chose their own way instead of God's way, the lights went out. Fellowship with God was broken and fellowship between people was confused. Inner peace fled and hearts went dark. Peace with the earth was confounded. The ground was cursed. Nature would never again work the way it was intended.

All the horrible realities in this world—from crazed men charging into schools with guns to the careless words we say that hurt our friends' feelings—it all flows from this.

And it flows through all of us. We've all been here. We went after an experience we thought would give life, and instead it brought shame. We've felt broken and isolated, and sensed that all is not as it should be. Aleksandr Solzhenitsyn, a Russian novelist and philosopher, once lamented, "If only there were evil people somewhere insidiously committing evil deeds and it were necessary only to separate them from the rest of us and destroy them. But the line dividing good and evil cuts through the heart of every human being."[3]

Though the traces of God's glorious designs are everywhere we look, nothing works quite right anymore. The virus of sin has corrupted every file of existence. And our greatest problem is precisely what the prophet Isaiah articulated to the Israelites: "Your iniquities have made a separation between you and your God" (Isaiah 59:2). We are in serious trouble. And unless someone comes to get us, we will never get out.

THE POOL OF EVIL

My grandmother used to have a pool in her backyard that had been emptied of water. Emptied of pool water, that is. Over the years it had been filled with rainwater. And sticks, and grass, and tree branches, and frogs, and snakes. And when you were a child with a vivid imagination, it was also filled with all things evil!

Now, what do you suppose a couple of young boys would do when their grandmother had a pool of evil in her backyard? Naturally, my brother and I would play on the edge of it.

One day when I was goofing around on the edge, I slipped and fell in. The surprise at falling quickly gave way to the terror of being trapped in that pool of evil—with all that lay lurking in it.

I got up and moved as fast as my little five-year-old legs could carry me to the shallow end, then attempted to leap up to grab the edge and pull myself out. But whoever had dug out that pool back in the day had been motivated. Even in the shallow end, I couldn't reach the ledge!

In my panic I looked up at my brother for help, but at six years old he had no strength to save me. So I engaged in the only other course of action available to a child: I cried.

I remember looking up through the wooden slats of the fence and seeing my grandmother's neighbor at the moment he heard my cries. I watched this young man, probably in his early twenties, drop the gardening tool he was working with and begin to run toward me. Then, in one single, fluid movement, he leapt over the entire fence. It was the coolest thing I had ever seen in my life. Without hesitation, he jumped down into that pool with me, and he lifted me out. He looked down at me and asked, "Are you alright?" I don't remember answering. But I do remember what I felt: awe. I was struck silent by the one who jumped into the chaos I had fallen into because of my own foolishness and brought me out.

This is exactly what Jesus Christ did for you and for me.

What was God's response in the garden when he saw sin break into the world? Did he demand that humanity clean itself up? No. He came up with a solution.

"The LORD God said to the serpent, . . . 'I will put enmity between you and the woman, and between your offspring and her offspring; *he* shall bruise your head, and you shall bruise his heel'" (Genesis 3:14–15).

Early church fathers considered this passage to be the first mention of the gospel in Scripture. God's answer to sin was that he would send a child to crush the one who deceived us. God's solution was a Savior who would destroy the one who hurt us.

HOW DID JESUS DESTROY THE WORK OF THE DEVIL?

John spoke of two ways that Jesus overcame the devil. The first was simply by his appearance (1 John 3:8). The arrival of Jesus on the planet was a landed invasion.

Do you know how his earthly ministry started? He was baptized by his cousin John in a public ceremony. The heavens opened and God declared, "This is my beloved Son," while the Spirit of God descended on him like a dove (Matthew 3:16–17). Right after that he was taken to the desert and confronted by the devil. As Satan attempted to dissuade Jesus from pursuing his mission, Jesus fended off each temptation with a quote from Deuteronomy. Satan even promised to give Jesus everything in the world if he would abandon God's work. Jesus flatly refused every offer of ease and ungodly power. He would not be deterred from his mission.

Jesus marched back to civilization "in the power of the Spirit" and headed to the synagogue in his hometown (Luke 4:14, 16). There he took up the writings of the prophet Isaiah, turned straight to the sixty-first chapter, and read aloud, "'The Spirit of the Lord is upon me, because he has anointed me to proclaim good news to the poor. He has sent me to proclaim liberty to the captives.' . . . Today this Scripture has been fulfilled in your hearing" (Luke 4:17–18, 21).

We know Jesus came to preach good news and care for the poor. But don't miss that third element of his call: to set the captives free!

Then he closed by saying, "This is being fulfilled in your presence right now!"

What did Jesus do next? He stepped out to wreak havoc on the darkness. He took disease away. He removed shame from women whose lives had been devastated sexually and relationally. He brought sanity back to a man who had been ravaged by dark and destructive forces. He brought life back into the home of a man who had driven people away through his ruthless pursuit of money. He mended what was broken in society. He wove peace into the world.

THE STRONGER ONE IS HERE

One of my favorite moments in Jesus' life is when he was asked to explain his ministry. He said, "When a strong man, fully armed, guards his own house, his possessions are secure. But when someone stronger than he attacks him and overpowers him, that man takes away his armor on which he had relied and distributes his plunder" (Luke 11:21–22 NASB).

Have you ever described Jesus in this way? As a strong guy who beats up another guy and steals his things? Yeah, well, that's how Jesus described himself.

Now, what does Jesus' story mean exactly? The armored man is the devil. The treasure is us. We were the possession of the strong one, right up until the Stronger One arrived to beat him up and set us free.

But isn't he the Prince of Peace?

You bet he is. And he's bringing peace through superior firepower.

Have you ever wondered why demons often ran off screaming when Jesus arrived on the scene? Jesus just gave you the answer. *The Stronger One is here.* His presence on the earth caused the world to go into a spiritual upheaval! Jesus walked into rooms, even places of worship, and people who had been tormented by the Enemy for years suddenly found themselves screaming in terror. The tyranny was at an end.

Let me stop right here and say this to you: I'm not sure what struggle or addiction or failure you're caught up in that's stealing your confidence and joy, but I'm going to tell you some good news. The Stronger One is here.

One of my favorite Jesus miracles was with the group of demons who, in the midst of their panic, asked, "Have you come here to torture us before the appointed time?" (Matthew 8:29 NIV). It's like they knew a whoopin' was coming; they just thought he was early!

As Jesus' career reached the climax, we see the Evil One make another move to disrupt his purposes. It was when Jesus divulged to his disciples that he had to march to Jerusalem to face rejection and death, and Peter strenuously objected. He rebuked Jesus for suggesting that he must go to the cross. Jesus did not respond directly to Peter, but rather to the source of the suggestion, saying, "Get behind me, Satan!" (Matthew 16:23). Jesus understood that the devil did not want him to get to that cross. Yet our Hero set his face "like a flint" toward Jerusalem, rode in as a king, and picked a fight with all the right people to get himself in serious trouble (Isaiah 50:7).

DESTROYING THE WORK OF SIN

Upon arrival in Jerusalem, Jesus declared to his disciples, "Now is the judgment of this world; now will the ruler of this world be cast out" (John 12:31). On the night he was betrayed, he said, "The ruler of this world is judged" (16:11). Then Jesus stepped out to destroy the devil, not by perpetrating an act of violence, but by taking violence upon himself.

The writer of Hebrews said it this way: "Since the children share in flesh and blood, He Himself likewise also partook of the same, so that through death He might destroy the one who has the power of death, that is, the devil, and free those who through fear of death were subject to slavery all their lives" (2:14–15 NASB).

He destroyed the work of sin by taking all its consequences upon himself. He took the thorns produced by the curse on the ground, the pain, sweat, and toil of work, the relational alienation from loved ones, and the brutal severing of fellowship with God.

Paul told Corinthian believers that "the sting of death is sin" (1 Corinthians 15:56). What makes death so poisonous is that we die guilty of transgressing God. He also said that "the power of sin is the law" (v. 56). What makes death so terrifying to us is that the law proves we are sinners and are guilty. But this is not where the story ends, Paul said: "Thanks be to God, who gives us the victory through our Lord Jesus Christ" (v. 57).

The greatest weapon the Enemy had against us was the truthful accusation that we are guilty and deserve judgment. So he "who knew no sin" knocked that weapon out of the Enemy's hands by becoming sin, so we could be right with God (2 Corinthians 5:21).

"He was pierced for our transgressions; he was crushed for our iniquities; upon him was the chastisement that brought us peace, and with his wounds we are healed" (Isaiah 53:5). The cross was his place of triumph over our Enemy. He took on our judgment and paid for it in full.

Colossians 2:13–15 says it this way:

When you were dead in your wrongdoings and the uncircumcision of your flesh, He made you alive together with Him, having forgiven us all our wrongdoings, having canceled the certificate of debt consisting of decrees against us, which was hostile to us; and He has taken it out of the way, having nailed it to the cross. When He had disarmed the rulers and authorities, He made a public display of them, having triumphed over them through Him. (NASB)

In the first century a triumph was an event, similar to a modern parade. When a king conquered an enemy in battle, the residents of the capital city organized a celebration. The king would ride into town on a white horse, met by the cheers of his grateful people. Behind him in the procession would be the vanquished enemy king. He was often stripped and shackled, put on display to show the people that they need not be afraid of him anymore. The final participants in the procession were the hostages who had been set free, marching triumphantly through the streets in white linen and swinging censers of burning incense. Those liberated by their victorious king filled the city with the sweet aroma of liberty.

Paul used this imagery to describe our lives in Christ: "Thanks be to God, who in Christ always leads us in triumphal procession, and through us spreads the fragrance of the knowledge of him everywhere" (2 Corinthians 2:14).

Notice the word *us*. This is the second way Jesus destroys the devil's work.

HIS APPEARING IN US

Another way Jesus destroys the work of the devil is by coming to reign in the individual human soul. First John 3:9 says, "No one born of God makes a practice of sinning, for God's seed abides in him; and he cannot keep on sinning, because he has been born of God." Sin is conquered—the work of the devil is destroyed—when a person is born of God. We move from lost to found. From orphaned to children of God. From the kingdom of darkness to the kingdom of the beloved Son.[4]

We become something new. And when that change of identity takes place, a change in activity will follow. John described this with the imagery of God's seed being in us. We are born again, and now we look like our Father.

Now, he wasn't saying we'd reach sinless perfection on earth. After all, he wrote in an earlier chapter, "If we say we have no sin, we deceive ourselves, and the truth is not in us. . . . If we say we have not sinned, we make him a liar, and his word is not in us" (1:8, 10). But the children of God do not revel in what their King gave his life to destroy; they're not content to live in ongoing, unrepentant sin.

When we are born of God there is a radical reorientation of our interactions with sin. The condemning power of sin is forever broken in our lives. We are no longer slaves! Our failures and shortcomings of the past no longer have the power to determine our future. Jesus has wiped away sin's penalty and will one day wipe out its very presence. This confidence in our new identity and secure destiny gives us the power to overcome the internal pull of our depravity.

Take a moment and step back in wonder at what our Conquering Warrior has accomplished. He came here on a mission to fight for us, and he succeeded.

We have truly been set free.

But we have not been set free from the fight. We have been set free *for* the fight.

FREE TO FIGHT

In the film *Master and Commander*, the captain of England's HMS *Surprise* engages the most dreaded frigate in Napoleon's navy in battle on the open sea. After disabling the ship's sails, the captain leads an assault team onto the bridge of the enemy vessel. They hack their way to the hold of the ship, where several sailors from other English ships are held in cages. In a pivotal scene, the captain breaks the chains and opens the prison door, and a soldier stands ready to hand each exiting man a sword.

The men are free . . . to step into a raging battle. Before, they were simply captives; now they have the chance to be conquerors.

This is our story.

Jesus has not only liberated us but also invited us to join the fight. C. S. Lewis explained, "Enemy-occupied territory—that is what the world is. Christianity is the story of how the rightful king has landed, you might say landed in disguise, and is calling us all to take part in his great campaign of sabotage."[5] We can feel like we are in a war because *we are in one*. Yet it is a war in which our King has won the decisive victory. Because he has been victorious, we can be too.

As I say this, I know many people who are so discouraged by their continuous fumbles and failures that they've begun to doubt that God has changed their lives. Maybe you feel like that. But what if I told you that your struggles, rather than being a sign of something wrong with you, are actually a sign of something right?

Picture a battlefield in the midst of the heat of a firefight. My mind goes to the gruesome scene on the beaches of Normandy during the D-Day landing of World War II. Amid the chaos of bombs detonating and bullets flying, there are two kinds of people on the field: The first type of person looks calm and still, unaffected by the destruction

WE HAVE NOT BEEN SET FREE FROM THE FIGHT. WE HAVE BEEN SET FREE <u>FOR</u> THE FIGHT.

surrounding them. The second type appears agitated. They're fighting a war within—battling fear, doubt, anxiety, terror—as the war wages without. What makes these two soldiers so different? The first person appears peaceful because he is dead. The deceased do not flinch when bullets strike the dirt. They don't duck as bombs erupt. The second person is aware of the battle because they are alive. It is the same spiritually.

The spiritually dead do not struggle with sin. Your struggles, far from being a sign of your spiritual death, are in fact just the opposite. Your struggle may be one of your greatest assurances that you are alive.

You are like those sailors in *Master and Commander* stepping off the enemy's boat, holding a sword. You have not been freed from your struggle against sin; you have been freed to struggle. Now you must learn how to struggle well.

One day not only sin's power but its very presence will be banished. We are not there yet, and until we get there we have a purifying work to do. We have a fight on our hands. And we are not left alone or unequipped! Jesus, our King, not only rescues us but also trains our hands for war.

CHAPTER 3

LIFE IN THE BATTLEFIELD

Several years ago I had the opportunity to observe a Navy SEAL assault training exercise. I watched the team approach and take over a building that was filled with enemy combatants who were holding hostages. Although this was a training exercise and they were using Simunition rounds (paintballs), they were fired from real guns. The rounds moved fast and hard, and they hurt. My understanding was that I would be watching from the safety of an observation deck.

However, as the team crept silently toward the building, the commanding officer motioned for me to follow him, and we began walking toward the front door. A few yards away he stopped abruptly and said, "I wouldn't get any closer if I were you. Sometimes when they blow the door the handle fires off like a bullet." I happily obliged. I hadn't planned on being that close in the first place!

Seconds later the door exploded and the team charged into the room. As soon as they did, the commanding officer tapped me on the chest and said, "Let's go." Then he went running behind his team into the building. I followed, charging in with them—wearing no protective gear or weapons, just my jeans and T-shirt. Super smart.

As I entered the room, two things immediately struck me (metaphorically speaking). The first was the *chaos of the situation*. Tight corners, shots firing, thick smoke, loud explosions—it was bedlam.

Yet in the midst of the confusion I was also struck by the *beauty of their strategy*. Aggressive yet graceful. Purposeful yet patient. Quick but controlled. Two men would approach an open hallway, then nod to each other and swing out in unison, instantly eliminating all threats while avoiding unnecessary exposure. In seconds they had neutralized the enemy, set free the hostages, and brought order to the chaos. I suddenly thought, *This is the Christian life!*

But you know what? Not everybody would agree with me on that.

I talk to many people who are surprised by their struggles. They're discouraged that they still wrestle with desires and temptations they thought would go away. Some even express disappointment in the gospel, as if the mission of Jesus has failed. *If he really did set me free, why do I still have this desire?* they wonder.

He did set you free. But he has not freed you *from* the struggle. He has freed you *to* struggle. Before, you were just a victim; now you have the possibility to be a victor. Jesus dramatically shifted your position! So now you must shift your perspective.

WHAT'S YOUR MENTALITY?

In this book, we're going to talk about changing your life, and you'll first need to believe change is possible. I know many of us pick up books like this because we know we need to change, but deep down inside we doubt that change is really possible for us. Maybe a few victories at the margins here and there, but a real, substantive shift to a life of purpose and meaning? That just seems out of reach. And it's because we feel the pull of our humanity.

Our beliefs undergird our behavior, and you need to believe that Jesus' mission didn't fail. God has done a great work inside you—a fundamental, internal change has happened! If the Master has laid his hands on you, you are not the same as you were before.

When Donna and I were newlyweds, we were given a dog, a beautiful, brindle-coat black mouth cur named Tiger. She was a total head case. She would run away from squirrels and hide from cats. If you reached out a hand to pet her, she would wince and pee on the floor.

We had been told that she'd been discarded in the woods by her previous owner, and over time we discovered that her master had been cruel. We did not hit her, we spoke kindly to her, and we took good care of her. But she was constantly reacting to her current, safe environment, including her new owners, with fear. She lived in a new reality but with an old mentality.

Her identity had changed from abused to loved, from discarded to adopted. Her position in life had shifted, so now she needed to shift her perspective.

Beliefs inform behaviors, and she had to decide to believe what was now true.

Over the course of a few months, we watched the implications of her new identity begin to impact her beliefs and activity. She quit wincing from our hands. She stopped fleeing from us. She began to rest.

Then she began to follow me around everywhere. She wanted to be near me. She would guard me like a sentry while I studied. She would sweep the perimeter of our home for signs of danger when we were hanging out in the backyard. She became the protector of our children and would leap in front of any snake, squirrel, or bird that appeared to be a threat. She owned her new identity and it began, over time, to shape her activity. Her position changed in a moment; her perspective and behavior changed through a process.

We have been given a new identity, and now we take up the process of working out the implications of this change in our lives.

This is where the fight begins. Our battle begins with belief.

PROGRESS AND STRUGGLE

Ephesians 2:1–2 tells us that we used to be dead in our sins, and when that was true of us, we "walked" in a lifestyle consistent with that lack of spiritual life. We followed the course of this world, the prince of the power of the air, and the passions of our flesh. We lived under God's condemnation, and we felt it.

But then God stepped in and did something decisive about it.

"God, being rich in mercy, because of the great love with which he loved us, . . . made us alive together with Christ . . . and raised us up with him and seated us with him" (vv. 4–6). This was entirely *his* work! "We are his workmanship, created in Christ Jesus for good works, which God prepared beforehand, that we should walk in them" (v. 10).

When we were dead, we walked like dead people. But now that we've been made new, we get to walk in a new way. Our new identity changes our activity forever.

We have before us the possibility of progress. John said it this way: "Beloved, we are God's children now, and what we will be has not yet appeared; but we know that when he appears we shall be like him, because we shall see him as he is. And everyone who thus hopes in him purifies himself as he is pure" (1 John 3:2–3).

We know that he who separated us from the penalty of sin will one day separate us from sin's very presence. That hope kickstarts a process of purification; we no longer revel in that which Jesus came to destroy. And that process will be marked by progress and struggle.

As we examine the nature of our struggle, this reality gives us comfort. Our assurance of salvation does not come from perfection, but from progress.

The first home Donna and I purchased had been abandoned for quite some time. This reality was instantly obvious in the condition of the yard. There was no grass. At all. But there were weeds—millions of them. Large, robust, angry weeds that grew over our heads. Tiny weeds that carpeted every inch of the lot. All manner of weeds flourished in this environment.

How do you think the neighbors discovered that a new resident had moved in? I took a Weed eater and I went to war! We tilled up the soil. We planted seeds and nourished the little sprouts of grass that began to rise. And as the months went by, there were less weeds and more grass.

Now, were all the weeds eliminated? My goodness, no. Was there a ton of grass growth? Again, no. In fact, if you were new to the neighborhood and just drove by the house six months after we had moved in, you might see the condition of the yard and assume that no one lived there. But you would be wrong, because you would have failed to see the progress over time.

The same is true of your heart and mine. How do we know that a new Resident has moved into our hearts? He begins to uproot former ways of thinking and living. He begins to plant new affections and inclinations. Will you suddenly be perfect? No. You will experience progress over time. Just remember that this progress involves struggle.

OUR ASSURANCE OF SALVATION DOES NOT COME FROM PERFECTION, BUT FROM PROGRESS.

RHYTHMS OF A WELL-FOUGHT LIFE

REST & WAR

AUTHORED BY BEN STUART

YOUR MISSION

When I was in elementary school we had two patrols. The first was the safety patrol, which directed traffic while students exited the school. (I'm not convinced it was a good idea to put fifth graders in charge of traffic!) The second was the fire patrol, which timed the evacuation drills and reported their findings to the school over the intercom (a *huge* deal when you're ten years old). While in fifth grade, with a little help from my brother and his friends, I was elected chief of the fire patrol at my elementary school. That meant that if a fire drill was conducted I had certain responsibilities to fulfill to ensure the safety of other students.

About a month into the school year, the alarm went off. I was sitting in math class and our teacher said, "Students, get in line and walk toward the back of the school." I was a student, so I got in line and began to file out like everybody else. I walked about midway down the hall when it hit me: *Wait a minute, I'm the fire chief. I shouldn't be going this way. The stopwatch is in the desk in the assistant principal's office at the front of the school!*

In that moment panic struck my little heart: *What should I do?* After a few seconds (which felt like an eternity), the crisis was resolved for me when I remembered the day the principal of our school appointed me fire chief. The highest authority in the school had given me a new identity, and that held more weight than the title of "student."

I stepped out of line. As little eyes around me widened in terror, I began to run the opposite direction. Feeling the stares of my entire class, I cried out as I sprinted, "I am the fire chief!"

We need to charge forward with our new identity and mission. Jesus declared war on the chaos of sin in order to bring us into the peace of his kingdom. The new identity he's given us comes with a whole new set of activities. We run a different way now. Our king has commissioned us to join him in the work of making war and cultivating rest.

YOUR STRATEGY

Now, as we're charging forward and running a different way, we need a clear strategy. Remember the story I told at the beginning of this chapter about the Navy SEALs' training exercise? We want to look more like the Navy SEALs and less like me. I was running into the fray wearing just my T-shirt and jeans, thinking, *It's smoky in here!* No weapon, no training, no clue what to do. But the SEALs burst in armed, trained, and ready to eliminate all threats and establish peace.

For those in Christ, the spiritual life is now one movement with two parts, *away* and *toward*:

1. We persistently move *away* from ways of thinking and living that discourage intimacy with God.
2. We continuously move *toward* ways of thinking and living that promote intimacy with God.

Theologians have historically called this movement *sanctification*. To sanctify something, or make it holy, means we set that thing apart. For example, in the Old Testament the temple had specific bowls and utensils that were holy unto God. This meant they were set apart from any common usage and dedicated only to tasks directly related to worshiping God.

Marriage could be thought of this way. Donna is holy unto me. That means she's set apart from an intimate relationship with any other guys (sorry, boys), and she is set apart only for intimacy with me. You may be sipping from a coffee mug right now that is holy unto you: no other lips may touch it.

Do you hear the two parts in that definition? To sanctify something means to set it apart *from* some things and set it apart *for* something. Away and toward.

The Scriptures present sanctification as both a particular event and an ongoing process. We were set apart to God when we put our faith in Jesus. The old life is gone and a new life has come. But far from simply being a past event, this new dynamic has opened us up to a present, ongoing process of being more and more set apart for only him.

Theologians in days past had words for each of these two parts: *mortification* and *vivification*. *Mortification* means I mortify, or put to death, certain ways of thinking and ways of living. I do not entertain them anymore. *Vivification* means there are other ways of thinking and living that I want to actively promote. I want to breathe life into them and see them grow and live and flourish.

This negative and positive combination could be illustrated with gardening: we must both pull weeds and plant flowers. Or it could be illustrated with dating. With my wife there are activities I do to promote intimacy: I take her on dates, we sit on the porch and talk about our thoughts and feelings, I write her notes. And there are activities I do not do: I don't speak harshly to Donna or date other women. I pursue activities that cultivate intimacy and I eliminate activities that would promote isolation.

Scripture tells us to "flee youthful passions and pursue righteousness, faith, love, and peace, along with those who call on the Lord from a pure heart" (2 Timothy 2:22). Do you see the two parts? We both flee and pursue.

We also read, "Let us also lay aside every weight, and sin which clings so closely, and let us run with endurance the race that is set before us, looking to Jesus, the founder and perfecter of our faith, who for the joy that was set before him endured the cross, despising the shame, and is seated at the right hand of the throne of God. Consider him who endured from sinners such hostility against himself, so that you may not grow weary or fainthearted" (Hebrews 12:1–3).

There are sins we need to cast off, and there is a race we are meant to run. We run this path with confidence because we know our Conquering Hero blazed the trail for us and will lead us home.

You could call it the big no and the big yes. Belonging to God brings with it a big no—there are things we no longer do, things that others we love may continue to do. But this is not all that spirituality entails. The big no is only half of the equation. The no opens you up to enjoy a better yes!

Now that we know what we are meant to do, we need to understand how to do it. We now have the big-picture *what*; next we need the details of *how*. How exactly do we flee and pursue? What does it look like? How do you know if you're doing it right?

In the next part of our journey, we will enter the war. We will explore the big no—moving away from whatever hinders enjoying God and fulfilling our purpose in him. After that, in part 3, we'll explore how to cultivate rest with God—the big yes.

Let's better understand the rhythms of the spiritual life God has for us: Eliminating and growing. Battling and building. Fleeing and pursuing. Defense and offense. Mortification and vivification. Rest and war.

PART 2

WAR WAR

CHAPTER 4

UNDERSTAND THE ENEMY'S PLAYBOOK

I remember my excitement on the morning of my first day of middle school. I walked to the bus stop in step with my big brother, who, by every measure, was endlessly cool. As we hopped onto the bus, he began to make his way to the back, where the cool kids sat. As his brother I knew I was cool by association, so I strode confidently toward the back as well. Suddenly, midway through my journey, a young man stood up from his seat in order to block my path. He put his face uncomfortably close to mine, attempting to stare me down.

"Are you Kole Stuart's brother?" he asked.

I said yes.

"I hate your brother," he whispered.

Okay. I guess you have the right to do that, I thought.

Then he continued, "So I hate you."

I discovered later that my new adversary, Marvin, was a bully. He derived some emotional value from picking on littler kids. There was just one problem: he had made a decision the previous year to play football. One day at practice he was on defense while my brother was on offense. My brother had caught the ball and begun to run to the goal line, and Marvin stepped in front of him in an attempt to make a tackle. My brother then proceeded to run full speed at Marvin and hit him so hard that Marvin flew through the air and landed flat on his back. Not only had Marvin flown through the air, but he made squealing sounds like a piglet on his way to the ground. This humiliation had severely cramped his style as a bully. It's hard to intimidate others when you've been publicly humiliated.

Fast-forward to our encounter on the bus. Marvin continued his speech: "I hate your brother . . . so I hate you." Then he put his finger directly under my eye and, while pushing on my face, said, "You'll look good with a cigarette burn right here."

At that moment my brother apparently turned to witness this encounter. I heard his voice boom from behind my adversary. "Marvin!"

My new nemesis jolted upright then quickly took his seat. But as I passed by him, he uttered the threat, "It's going to be a long year, little brother."

Now, let me ask you a question. Why did this young man hate me? I had not personally done anything to him. I will tell you why: I looked like the one who'd shamed him.

If you are now associated with Christ, the Enemy hates you. Why? Because you look like the One who humiliated him. As the seventeenth-century minister William Gurnall once said, "It is this image of God reflected in you that so enrages hell; it is this at which the demons hurl their mightiest weapons."[1]

The apostle Paul told us that our Hero made a public spectacle of the devil when he triumphed over him on the cross (2 Corinthians 2:14; Colossians 2:15). The devil is hopelessly outmatched by the power of our Conquering Hero. But he has one tactic left: he can come after the little brothers and sisters of the King.

We have an enemy. And before we consider the strategy we'll take with him, we must first analyze his.

ANALYZING THE PLAYBOOK

There is a great scene in the movie *Patton* where General George S. Patton faces off against the Nazis' most feared general, Erwin Rommel. Known as the Desert Fox, Rommel had literally written the book on modern tank warfare. The movie sets up the dramatic tension: How will the untested Patton hope to survive before the might of Rommel and his German panzers? What proceeds is a rout. The US II Corps completely destroys the Nazi army led by their great general. In the moment of triumph, the camera pans to the victorious Patton as he surveys the battlefield. Then Patton cries out, "Rommel . . . I read your book!"[2]

Do you want victory over your spiritual Enemy? You must first understand how he comes at you. So let's read his playbook. Specifically, let's look at his goals, what he knows, and what he does.

Our Enemy's goal is to get you and me to sin. He wants us willfully engaging in activities that dishonor our Lord, distance us relationally from him, diminish our power to pursue our created purpose, and ultimately prove to be self-destructive.

He cannot succeed in any kind of direct assault against the Almighty, but he can grieve God's heart by convincing God's children to distrust and disobey him, the One who gave his all for them. The best way to twist the knife in our King is to convince us to rebel against him by participating in acts that dishonor him and steal our joy. How could the Enemy possibly accomplish this? Why would we go along with it? Let's analyze what he knows.

What he knows is *you*. He has studied your movements. He has observed your ways. He has watched the game film on you. Specifically he knows two things: your wiring and your tendencies.

THE ENEMY KNOWS YOUR WIRING

By *wiring* I mean he knows that we are comprised of the mind, affections, and the will. We have a mind that is constantly engaged in a cognitive process, regularly interacting with ideas and reasoning. Additionally we possess a heart that feels deeply. Our affections respond to information by being inclined either toward it or adverse to it. And our will is our internal drive to act. Though there are more sophisticated ways of speaking of our internal wiring, these simple categories help us understand what is happening inside us as we engage with the world. We think, we feel, we act.

And these elements interact. Our thoughts provide the fuel for the fire of our emotions. Our affections drive our decisions. Our will feels the heat from our affections, and then we act.

In the New Testament these three parts of our inner life—the mind, the affections, and the will—are often lumped together and spoken of as our "heart" or "the inner person." For our purposes we will speak of the mind, affections, and will.

My main point here is that the Enemy is aware that we are wired this way. But this is not all he knows. He also knows each of our particular tendencies.

THE ENEMY KNOWS YOUR TENDENCIES

By *tendencies* I mean our personal inclinations toward certain ideas or behaviors. He knows our particular proclivities—the unique, individual ways we are prone to react to something.

When I watched the Netflix documentary *The Social Dilemma*, I learned of the massive amounts of data harvested by tech companies about everyone who is regularly online. Every action you take on a computer or through an app is carefully recorded, stored, and analyzed. Tristan Harris, a former Google employee who now leads the Center for Humane Technology,[3] explained that so much data has been collected on you that they can predict your decisions and actions with stunning accuracy.

This data is then used to market targeted products that you are most likely to buy, or articles and posts on which you are most likely to click. One example he gave was how a company will know that on a certain month of the year you are more likely to go to old photos of an ex-lover and listen to sad music. So in that particular month the company will send you reminders of those photos and recommendations of melancholy music. Your behavior has been studied so that it can be influenced.[4]

The devil does the same thing. He knows your hopes, dreams, longings, inclinations, and vulnerabilities. He knows you and how to influence you.

Embedded in that knowledge is the understanding that there is still a part of you that longs for what Jesus came to destroy. We are like Gollum in *The Lord of the Rings*, who both loves and hates the ring. We know sin destroys us, but an insane part of us still longs to indulge in that which kills us. We are addicts to our particular flavors of depravity. We are prone to wander; Lord, we feel it.

THE ENEMY'S STRATEGY

So the devil is armed with this information; what then is his strategy? How does he work? In order to convince us to willfully participate in insane acts of self-sabotage, he knows he must suggest certain thoughts that will stir our affections—so that we will enact our will. The Scriptures have a single word to describe this moment he works hard to manufacture: *temptation*.

Now, you may ask, "Ben, where are you getting this from?" I got it from James, the brother of Jesus, who said, "Each person is tempted when he is lured and enticed by his own desire. Then desire when it has conceived gives birth to sin, and sin when it is fully grown brings forth death" (James 1:14–15).

The word *lure* in the text speaks of attracting your mind's attention. The word *entice* describes stirring your affections. You have entered into temptation when certain thoughts are solicited to your mind in order to stir your affections toward an activity that's self-destructive and dishonoring to God, enticing you to enact your will to choose it.

Let's take a minute to focus in on the word *lure*. When you fish, what do you do out there on the water? You cast out your line to present a lure before a fish. What is your hope? You want to capture that fish's attention. Maybe you use a lure that looks like a frog, and you bob it along the surface of the lake so it will look wounded and delicious. You don't just want that fish's attention. You want to stir his affections! You want to interrupt him midsentence with his other fish buddies! You want him to turn and say, "Hello there, little frog. You are looking scrumptious today." When his attention is effectively captured and his affections properly stirred, he'll enact his will and bite down on that lure—and you've got him. He never even saw the hook. He was completely unaware that there was a sentient being behind the whole experience, exploiting his desires for malevolent ends.

Now, some fish may not take that bait. They may see your frog and think, *A frog . . . really? That's gross.* They may stare incredulously at the fish who are drawn in by it. *That turns you on? Ew. I can't believe a real fish would be attracted to that.*

That's okay. You just attach a different lure, maybe something shiny that it finds irresistible. We aren't all attracted to the same lures. But there's a lure out there for each of us. James said that "each person is tempted." There are tailor-made temptations for all of us. Some of the best self-knowledge you can have is knowing how the Enemy lures you.

Ladies, imagine you are getting ready in the morning and the thought is solicited to your mind, *I am single.* As you contemplate this sentence, your mind reasons: *This is true. I am neither married nor currently dating anyone.* Yet as this thought consults your affections, your heart cries out, *But I don't want to be alone. I want to be with someone.*

A love song comes on and that yearning for connection comes rising up from the depth of you with greater force. As you drive to work, you see couples walking hand in hand. You see birds flying two by two. The thought rises to your mind, *Everyone has someone but me!*

Then, while you are in that state, you receive a proposition . . . and you date a loser. He is someone who is beneath you morally. You know his priorities do not align with those of Jesus, your King. But you begin to believe that he is the best you can do. And in time, you end up in a relationship and a series of tragic events you were never meant to be in.

Gentlemen, imagine you are getting ready in the morning and the thought crosses your mind, *You should think about naked people.* Your affections cry out, *Naked people—sounds great!* And your screen of choice offers you an endless supply of unclothed skin.

The devil understands this basic concept: What you think about, you will care about. What you care about, you will chase.

BE A STUDENT OF YOURSELF

Awareness is our first and most important response to an attack. What holds my attention? Why? What is stirring my affections? Why does it entice me so? What am I being tempted to do exactly? Sometimes I say it out loud. Deception dies in the light. Drag it out into the open. Be curious about yourself. Be a student of yourself. Awareness is the first step in effective action.

The apostle Paul implored his young protégé Timothy, "Keep a close watch on yourself and on the teaching. Persist in this, for by so doing you will save both yourself and your hearers" (1 Timothy 4:16). He told him to keep watch on his teaching, or his doctrine. *Know what you believe, Timothy.*

But notice he also told him to keep a close watch on himself. *Know yourself, Timothy. Be a student of your own wiring and tendencies.*

He told him to persist in this. *Be vigilant.*

There was an important incentive for Timothy: by developing these habits he would keep both himself and everyone he influenced from destruction.

How many of us have been hurt by a spiritual leader whose moral failures discouraged our faith and disrupted our hope? How many times have you been wounded by a mentor's ignorance of their own lusts?

Before we judge them too harshly, let's take a good look at ourselves. Sometimes it is easy to see this destructive dynamic play out in others' lives while we are blinded to it in our own.

In his brilliant treatise *Of Temptation: The Nature and Power of It*, John Owen warned, "He . . . who is not exactly skilled in the knowledge of himself, will never be disentangled from one temptation or another all his days. . . . Uselessness and scandal in [believers] are

WHAT YOU THINK ABOUT, YOU WILL CARE ABOUT. WHAT YOU CARE ABOUT, YOU WILL CHASE.

RHYTHMS OF A WELL-FOUGHT LIFE

REST & WAR

AUTHORED BY BEN STUART

branches growing constantly on this root of unacquaintedness with their own frame and temper."[5]

Are you "exactly skilled" in the knowledge of yourself? Are you deeply acquainted with your own proclivities? What thoughts come to mind when you are tired? What activities seem rational when you are angry? What are your go-to comforts when you are lonely or feel discouraged? Observe your own movements so you can know yourself better. Be a student of yourself.

In the classic manual on warfare, *The Art of War*, Sun Tzu declared, "If you know the enemy and know yourself, you need not fear the result of a hundred battles. . . . If you know neither the enemy nor yourself, you will succumb in every battle."[6]

Let's not allow ourselves to be in a position where we'll end up succumbing in every battle.

As we've said before, the question is not whether we are in a spiritual battle. Open war is upon us, friends.[7] The only question remaining is whether we will choose to struggle well.

We know the Enemy's strategy now. Next, we can start working on our own.

RHYTHMS OF WAR

1. Write out 1 Timothy 4:16 in a journal.
2. Take a moment to consider what you think about. What topics, subjects, and ideas float into your mind most frequently? What do your thoughts linger on most naturally?
3. Think about what you care about. What subjects elicit the strongest emotional responses from you? What excites you? What bums you out?

| | | | | | | | | | | | | | | | | | | | | | | | | | | | | | | | | | | | | | | | | | | | | | | | | | | | | | | | | | | | | | | | | | |

1   2   3   4   ⑤   6   7   8   9   10   11   12   13   14   15

▲

CHAPTER 5

ELIMINATE EXPOSURE

"Floyd Mayweather Jr.: A Master at Not Getting Hit," read the *Wall Street Journal* headline.[1]

It was no exaggeration.

Mayweather ended his professional boxing career with a staggering record of fifty wins and zero losses. How does a man enter the ring that many times with trained fighters and never walk out with a loss? He landed roughly 46 percent of his punches thrown at his opponents, while they managed to get only 22 percent on him. In his prime his adversaries only landed 16 percent of punches thrown—no other boxer's stats have even come close to that number!

Mayweather cemented his legacy as a boxing legend for one simple reason: the man knew how not to get hit. The secret to his success can be reduced to a consideration of time and place. If you don't want to get hit, don't be there when the punch arrives!

The same principle holds true for us as we contemplate our strategy with the Enemy. If we want to spend less time rocked by guilt and staggered by shame, then we need to reduce our exposure to the *whens* and *wheres* of temptation. As football coach Paul "Bear" Bryant used to say,

"Defense wins championships."[2] Our first strategy to thwart the Enemy requires that we identify and eliminate the moments of temptation.

In Matthew 26:41 Jesus advised his disciples, "Watch and pray that you may not enter into temptation." Notice he did not say enter into *sin*, but into *temptation*—the moment when our minds are persistently solicited and our affections constantly stirred by inferior desires. To avoid sin we must avoid temptation. This is where Jesus draws the battle line.

ANALYZE THE MOMENT

Years ago a friend told me the story of a buddy of his who came to him in great distress. His friend confided in him that he was consistently arguing with his wife and that their disagreements had escalated into explosive altercations. My friend asked the man if he could retrace the moments that led to their arguments.

After thinking for a while, the man explained that they typically happened on nights they spent at their local bar. They would drink excessively with the community there and, inevitably, some men would make suggestive comments toward his wife. In his estimation she did not rebuff their advances enough. This would make him feel jealous. He would accuse her of encouraging them, and she would respond defensively. The argument would continue, and often escalate, as they arrived home.

My friend told him there were likely deeper issues they needed to address and should do so in counseling. However, in the short-term, he advised the man to stop going to that bar. If that moment—drinking excessively in that crowd—consistently led to marital strife, then they should eliminate it.

The suggestion caught the man off guard. It appeared he had never considered that option. "But it's Tequila Tuesday," he said.

Who cares?! If that moment always leads to a destructive one, eliminate that moment.

I counseled a young couple who were dating and wanting to abstain from sex until marriage. They came to me in distress because they had set some healthy physical boundaries in their relationship but found they could not keep them. Multiple times they had violated their own standards and woke up the next day feeling ashamed. I asked them if they could pinpoint what events led up to their moments of compromise.

They thought for a moment. Then it hit them. It always seemed to happen on nights they watched a movie together in one of their apartments. The night always began with the two of them seated upright on the couch facing the screen and ended with them horizontal together on the couch.

I told them, "If you aren't tempted in that moment, you have a whole different set of problems!" It completely makes sense that lingering in a dimly lit room alone with someone you are extremely sexually attracted to ends in sexual activity.

If you can relate to this couple, then I'll tell you what I told them next: "If you want purity, you need to eliminate that moment. And that's a decision you need to make long before you enter that environment, while you still have your wits about you."

MAKE NO PROVISION

When Donna and I were dating, we decided early on never to be alone with each other in an apartment. She was hot! Of course I wanted to touch her. But I also wanted to withhold sexual intimacy until I was ready to unite every aspect of our lives together in the covenant of marriage. So I told her, "Apartments aren't evil. Movies aren't evil. But if you get me in that environment alone with you, *I* might get evil. So let's go on a date to a crowded restaurant where I am much less likely to want to grope you!"

I have counseled several young men who struggle deeply with an addiction to pornography. (I know that an increasing amount of young women do as well, about 33 percent, but my counseling experience has been exclusively with men.[3]) I always ask them some version of this question: When and where do you feel most tempted? Describe in detail the moments when you succumb to the temptation. Many confide in me that they view porn on their phones late at night alone in their rooms. I've encouraged them to get their phones away from their beds. Analyze the moment for a second: you are putting an incredible source of temptation right next to your head when you are in your most weary and vulnerable state. That is a perfect recipe for disaster.

Paul exhorted the Romans, "Make no provision for the flesh in regard to its lusts" (Romans 13:14 NASB). Positioning a temptation source within arm's reach is giving your flesh *ample* provision. That's like an alcoholic pouring a glass of scotch every night, setting it on the nightstand, and declaring, "Now, I'm not going to drink you." It's a bad strategy.

Some will push back, saying, "But I use my phone as my alarm clock."

Then get a separate alarm clock! It is not worth sinning over. If there is a mix of factors that constantly leads you into temptation, you need to change the variables. If you do not like the outcomes, analyze the inputs. Eliminate the moment.

IF YOU DO NOT LIKE THE OUTCOMES, ANALYZE THE INPUTS. ELIMINATE THE MOMENT.

We had a young lady in our ministry years ago who confessed to one of our staff that she had been cutting herself. As we helped her discover what thoughts led her to take such actions, our team discovered that she had filled her room with images from fashion magazines of impossibly attractive women. Now, there were obviously some deeper identity and self-worth issues that needed to be addressed. But one of the first steps our staff took was helping her change her room. Surrounding herself with an impossible standard of beauty had fed her insecurities about her own body, and in her despair she began to believe cutting herself was the only way to find relief from her emotional torment.

This art of eliminating the moment of temptation requires awareness not only of ourselves but also of our environment. Psychologist Kurt Lewin once observed that "behavior is a function of a person in an environment."[4] We must develop situational awareness. Then we can move from awareness to avoidance.

THE ART OF WAR

Years ago when I read Sun Tzu's *The Art of War*, I was surprised how little the author wrote about the actual moment of battle. Much of his attention focused on positioning troops in advantageous environments and avoiding compromising ones. The book is filled with lines like:

- "When in difficult country, do not encamp."[5]
- "Do not linger in dangerously isolated positions."[6]
- "Do not move up-stream to meet the enemy. . . . In crossing salt-marshes, your sole concern should be to get over them quickly, without any delay."[7]

The master strategist understood that success depends largely upon knowledge of your surroundings.

We must give this level of attention to our lives as well, and for good reason.

In his book *Atomic Habits*, James Clear explained that cues in our environment kickstart cravings inside of us. Once the craving starts, we respond by moving to satisfy it. Our cravings intensify with increased exposure to those cues.[8] *If we want to decrease the power of a craving, then our first line of defense must be to minimize the cues in our environment.*

So many people I counsel beat themselves up over their lack of willpower to resist certain temptations. While internal fortitude is vital for a victorious life, sometimes we need to focus on having more forethought. If we can recognize the moment temptation begins and eliminate it, then less willpower will be required.

Many of our most disappointing actions could be eliminated by intentionally designing our environment. Do you miss morning workouts because you are too tired? Research shows that screen time disrupts sleep time, so try removing all screens from your bedroom. Do you constantly lose time to social media while at work? Put your phone out of arm's reach. Do you mindlessly overeat? Get all the junk food out of your house.

Take a moment to consider the circumstances in which you consistently compromise. Where are you? When is it? Who are you with? Have you allowed yourself to linger in dangerously isolated positions? Ask yourself, *Are there places I should no longer go? Are there certain times of the day or the week when I am particularly vulnerable to certain temptations? How can I move myself to a more secure environment in those moments?*

Many of the people who check into rehab facilities for addictions find they can get and stay sober in that supportive and structured environment. But if they return to the same house, neighborhood haunts, and friendship groups where they'd previously acted out, they relapse. Their sobriety depends largely upon altering their surroundings.

Think of how the same principles apply to you. Become mindful of where you move, when you move, and who you move with. Know that your context will shape your character.

LEGALISM VS. WISDOM

Some might quip, "Ben, really? Eliminate *all* the moments that lead to temptation? Doesn't this sound a bit like legalism?"

Let me be clear: what I am advocating is not legalism but wisdom. I do not have a blanket list of rules for everyone; I am offering guiding principles you can adapt to the realities of your own life. You must know yourself and where you are weak. This is wise.

I have friends who have struggled with an addiction to alcohol and have realized they cannot spend any time at a bar. The sights, sounds, and smells all conspire to kickstart an insatiable urge within them to drink. They have tried to hang out with friends and remain sober in those environments, but over time it has proven to be unwise. It is a moment that more often than not has led to compromise. So, for their own health, they choose not to go there anymore.

For others, walking into a bar produces no temptation. They can meet a friend for a drink after work and feel no wild impulse to continue drinking through the night. An hour in a bar does not light the fuse of an inevitable explosion of failure.

I had a friend who spent years as a designated driver for his college buddies. He was the one they knew they could call and ask to come pick them up, because their haunts held no allure for him.

But that same friend had been waging a long battle against his struggle with pornography. In his ongoing war with lust, he had eliminated many of his online portals, but he found that, in moments of desperation, he would wander through bookstores and look for books or magazines with illicit images. They didn't incite as much lust as what he found online, but still, there was a little rush. This rush, though, came with a big risk; it was usually the first step down a road that led him to further and more substantial compromise. So for him, bars were not a problem, but he realized he should no longer go to his local bookstore.

This is what I mean by wisdom, not legalism. For some of us wisdom looks like visiting bookstores, but not bars. For others, it may mean bars, but no bookstores. We must be honest with ourselves.

ENVIRONMENT OF THE MIND

You may say, "Ben, these illustrations are sort of helpful, but my greatest temptations rise not from a physical environment, but from an onslaught of negative thoughts."

I get that. You could be walking down the street or driving in your car and suddenly feel overwhelmed by an assault of lustful, resentful, or despairing thoughts. How can you eliminate those temptations if the environment is your mind? This is an important topic and we will address it more later in this book. For now let's just focus on a principle that came up in the last chapter: what you think about will determine what you care about and inform what you chase.

At the time of this writing, Americans on average spend more than seven hours a day staring at screens—computers, smartphones, televisions, tablets.[9] Some of us whittle the hours away watching videos of cute dogs or home improvement tips. But much of what we find online consists of distortions of sex, the glamorizing of violence, and the constant terror of impending tragedy gleefully reported in the news. When we consider this reality, it becomes easier to understand why we feel constantly entangled by fear, lust, and pride. Our inputs determine our outcomes. And when we soak our minds in chaos, our lives begin to reflect the same.

When you hike up a mountain, how do you get to the top? One step at a time. The accumulation of little steps leads to a destination. We have slowly and imperceptibly wandered off the paths of peace. If every wicked act is powered by distorted affections, and every distorted affection is fueled by destructive thoughts, then we must work to feed our mind with different input.

It starts with awareness: Where are we directing our attention? What do we allow our mind to entertain? Then we ask, what different tools might we employ to forcefully change the subject in our minds?

It is important to note here that the solicitation of inappropriate thoughts to your mind is not your fault. You cannot always help what thoughts enter your mind, but you can choose what you entertain. When you allow a thought to linger and invite it to parlay your heart—this is where you get into trouble. The solicitation is not evil, but entertaining the thought and acting on it is.

Peter told believers, "Do not be conformed to the passions of your former ignorance" (1 Peter 1:14). Their distorted passions led to destructive practices. He instructed them to discontinue this life by "preparing [their] minds for action, and being sober-minded" (v. 13).

THE DEVIL PLAYS CHESS

Eighteenth-century theologian Jonathan Edwards declared in his resolutions: "Resolved, whenever I do any conspicuously evil action, to trace it back, till I come to the original cause; and then both carefully endeavor to do so no more, and to fight and pray with all my might against the original of it."[10]

Whenever we experience temptation, we do well to trace it back to its first impulse. Look at the moments that led to the moment of temptation and the moment of failure. This takes intentional thought because the devil is a master strategist.

A great chess player knows he cannot win the game in a single move. He also knows he cannot be too obvious about his intentions. So he mentally plans out ten or twelve moves before he makes his first one. He devises a strategy to subtly shift the pieces on the board over time so that, unbeknownst to you, he has slowly and imperceptibly decreased your ability to resist his advance.

The Enemy works the same way. He knows he cannot get many of us to succumb to a temptation with one or two solicitations. We are too smart for that. He doesn't come to you at midday when you are at peak strength and say, "Let's begin an opioid addiction today, shall we?" He plays chess. He'll start with some irritations early in the day. Then add a setback at work, sprinkle in some negative and cynical thoughts, and begin to whisper enticements. He'll push you toward sin with resentments, then pull you toward it with enticements. Then suddenly a way of acting that seemed unthinkable a few hours earlier now seems acceptable.

He knows he cannot beat you in two moves. So he works to beat you in twelve.

One of my seminary professors told the story of a young man

speaking to his doctoral board. While discussing his spiritual life, he confessed to his mentors that he struggled with an addiction to pornography. They asked him some questions about the nature of the circumstances leading up to his addictive behaviors.

He said to his professors, "If I'm honest, it starts months before the moment I act out. I have homework to do and I procrastinate. I feel shame about that, but I ignore the shame and distract myself with mindless surfing online or time with friends. As the workload piles up, I start to feel not only shame but also stress. I feel overwhelmed. Then as the deadlines approach, I work late into the night to get everything done. So I sleep less. I mindlessly snack while staying up late. So my body feels bad and I feel shame about my health choices. And it is in that environment—feeling unhealthy, stressed, ashamed, and tired—that suddenly the urge to look at porn rises with force. I enter into temptation."

He then explained that he'd discovered a successful strategy in the war on his porn addiction: not to simply wait until the moment that the temptation was at its full strength and then try to resist. Instead, he planned ahead by buying a calendar at the beginning of every semester. In that calendar he scheduled out his days, including set times to study and do schoolwork. If he kept a consistent rhythm of studying, he did not need to let work, stress, shame, and exhaustion all pile up—and let temptation rise. One of the best weapons against his war on lust was a day planner bought six months before any temptation might rise.

It is easier to resist the river of temptation when it is a tiny stream, not a raging waterfall. It's better to battle an army while they're putting on their armor and trying to find their weapons than when they're armed and charging toward you.

Keep way ahead of temptation, and you'll gain a huge advantage.

RESIST THE FIRST IMPULSE

One of the most effective martial arts practiced today is jujitsu. It involves a fighter using his body to isolate and trap a part of his opponent's body. By using leverage he can then break the person's bone, snap a tendon, or, if he's isolated his neck, squeeze him until he passes out. The term *jujitsu* means "the gentle art."[11] A jujitsu master grips tightly onto you and slowly, gently, and methodically squeezes you into submission.

In an interview with *GQ* magazine, Georges St-Pierre, one of the greatest mixed martial artists of all time, was asked how he managed to escape and defeat so many jujitsu artists throughout his career. He explained that for every possible submission hold there exists an effective counter technique. There is always a means of escape. However, he then strongly qualified that statement by explaining that the longer you allow an opponent to grip you, the harder it becomes to escape. The longer they can impose their will, the more they can weaken your resolve. Thus the best moment to apply your counter technique is at the first sign of a submission attempt. If you want victory, you must move swiftly and decisively at the first sign of the enemy's squeeze.[12]

Likewise, it is best for us to resist temptation at its first impulse.

In Proverbs 5, the writer warned his son of the dangers of adultery. He described in shocking detail the alluring thoughts that precede the act, then said, "Keep your way far from her, and do not go near the door of her house, lest you give your honor to others and your years to the merciless" (vv. 8–9). Notice he did not say, "*While you're in bed with her*, take a moment to consider the wisdom of this activity." He told him to avoid the very door of her house!

Center the energy of your attack on the moment of temptation. Do not wait until you're in her house, on the couch, or in the bedroom. Don't let temptation get momentum and then try to stop its progress. Better not to even get anywhere near the door of her house, because you know where that ultimately leads, and it is not where you want to end up.

In my early days of ministry, a young man approached me while I was locking up our church offices. He came running up, out of breath, carrying a desktop computer. "Take this," he said.

"Um, I'm not sure I can do that," I replied. "Where did you get this?"

He was hesitant to get into details and just asked, "Would you just be willing to store it in your office for a few days?"

"Are you asking me to be an accomplice in something?" I questioned.

Finally, he confessed that the computer was his. With a look of embarrassment, he explained that his parents were leaving town for the weekend. A recovering porn addict, he knew what would happen. He would try to muster willpower to avoid the allure of the screen, but as his resolve wore down, he would compromise. So he'd decided on a new tactic. The moment his parents left the house, he'd unplugged the computer and drove up to the church, determined to hand it off to whoever he encountered.

I told him he should not feel embarrassed at all. What he did was wise. I will never forget the look of relief and joy on his face as he walked away. He fought the temptation early and was able to enjoy the sweet taste of a victory.

I have never fought a lion, but if I had to, I'd rather face a baby one. Do you see what I'm getting at here? Don't wait until the predator grows to its full height before you wage war. Better to fight the beast when it's small.

Remember Jesus warned his disciples to watch and pray that they may not "enter into" temptation (Matthew 26:41). The greatest way to exit a compromising environment is to never enter it to begin with!

John Owen, in his classic work *The Mortification of Sin*, warned, "Be always awake that you may have an early discovery of your temptation. . . . Die rather than yield one step to it. Thou hadst never had the experience of the fury of sin, if thou hadst not been content with some of its dalliances."[13] If you start to give it space in your affections, it will arrive in your actions.

REDRAW YOUR BATTLE LINES

Take a moment and think about where you might need to redraw the battle lines in your life. You may need to remove some screens from prominent places in your home and eliminate the temptation to spend hours online. Maybe you need to get a calendar so you can better schedule your days and avoid the familiar path of procrastination, frustration, temptation.

I have friends who've been able to avoid their addictive behaviors by drawing the battle line at their resentments. If they coddle resentments in their hearts and hold on to all the little slights and letdowns from the day, a buildup of frustration will become an internal pressure longing for release. The next thing they know, there will be a voice of entitlement in their mind saying, *You deserve a break*, and the pull of temptation will get an assist from the push of their resentments. They've realized they have to keep watch of resentments and deal with them before they build up. To avoid relapse, they have to daily, prayerfully release them.

Once you find that you have the power to resist, it will become easier the next time. You'll grow a bit and your lust will shrink. It may not completely disappear in this life, but you can, over time, reduce its power.

We are told in Romans 6 that our old self was crucified so we would no longer be slaves to sin. We can think of fighting our temptations as though we are crucifying our "old self" desires. John Owen used a vivid and disturbing illustration of crucifixion that's fitting here. He said that no one likes to be crucified; they will kick and scream and rage as you place them on the wood. Then as they are forced to remain there and they slowly bleed out, they will lose their power to resist.[14] Like I said, gruesome. But it is a good illustration of your sin. When you resist a temptation, the broken inner part of you will scream out in resistance. And if you keep that "old self" on the cross, it will lose its vitality. Your resolve will grow strong as your lusts grow weak.

NUDGE AND SWAY

Remember when we talked about boxer Floyd Mayweather's successful defensive strategy? Its effectiveness rested in large part on his attention to details that may have been imperceptible to the untrained eye. He would tuck his chin to reduce the possibility of his opponent landing a knockout punch. He'd narrow his shoulders and lower his left hand to protect his body from attack. He would slightly roll his shoulder, and, in doing so, greatly reduce the size of his target. His awareness of his body position prevented attacks from ever landing, giving him the "ability to facilitate his offense using his defense."[15] One of his opponents, Ricky Hatton, remarked in an interview, "He was so clever defensively and it would just be a little nudge or sway that made all the difference."[16]

A little nudge or sway makes all the difference. True for Floyd, and true for us. What are some nudges and sways in your life you need to make to reduce your target for temptations? What subtle shifts might position you for greater success?

As you consider your answer, keep this in mind: Jesus told his disciples to watch and be attentive to their inner life and external environment. He told them to pray and invite God into that process of living with more intentionality. He also encouraged them to invite others into it and engage in the pursuit together. "Watch and pray" is a communal command (Matthew 26:41).

Often our darkest thoughts arrive and grow strongest when we are isolated. Jesus invites us to interrupt that moment with the arrival of conversation with trusted friends and with God himself. Sometimes a simple moment of intercession to God can be sufficient to stop the forward progression of temptation or keep you away from it altogether.

RHYTHMS OF WAR

1. In your journal, write out Matthew 26:41 in its entirety.
2. Take a moment and think about a bad habit or besetting sin that you need to eliminate. What is the temptation you consistently find yourself entering into? Consider writing it down.
3. How could you design your environment to reduce your exposure to that temptation? Write out a few practical steps you can take.

CHAPTER 6

PADDLE DOWNSTREAM

The anticipation was palpable. The Buffalo Wild Wings felt electric as hundreds of us were packed together. Only moments before, we'd been strangers, and now we were sharing tables and talking loudly together over the din of the crowd. We all brought different ethnicities, backgrounds, careers, and religious beliefs to the room, but we were all there for one united purpose: to see who would win the rematch between Georges St-Pierre and B. J. Penn.

Their first mixed martial arts battle had been declared a split decision in St-Pierre's favor. Avid vans of Penn protested, pointing to St-Pierre's bloodied face at the end of the fight compared to Penn's lack of damage. So when the moment they would again face off finally arrived, opinions were strong, battle lines were drawn, and excitement was through the roof.

The first round was evenly matched. St-Pierre, the superior wrestler, kept pressing Penn against the cage. He appeared to be attempting to take Penn down to the mat but was unsuccessful. As St-Pierre would lean his body onto Penn and attempt to grab his hips to throw him,

Penn would pull him back upward and push his body away. The first round was inconclusive.

But then something strange happened. As the subsequent rounds wore on, St-Pierre's takedown attempts were successful. He could bulldoze through Penn's defenses and put him on the mat. Next, something even more shocking took place. When St-Pierre didn't take the fight to the ground, he beat Penn in striking while on the feet too. As the superior striker, Penn had been favored by most commentators to dominate the stand-up game. But as the fight wore on, St-Pierre beat him on every level, until finally Penn's trainers threw in the towel.

In the post-fight interview, reporters eagerly questioned St-Pierre about how he had managed to so thoroughly defeat an opponent who had previously caused him problems. They asked how he overcame the discouragement of his unsuccessful takedown attempts in the first round.

St-Pierre responded by saying he actually *hadn't wanted* to take down Penn. St-Pierre knew if he could just keep attempting takedowns, Penn would have to pull his body up and push it away. This would fill Penn's distinctively small shoulders with blood and fatigue them, which would eventually slow down his punches—thus rendering his most effective weapon useless. This was the brilliance of St-Pierre's strategy: his goal in round one was to sap his opponent's power so it would become easier for St-Pierre to avoid his punches later on.

In the previous chapter we considered how to reduce our exposure to moments of temptation. However, even when we're careful about avoiding temptation, there will still be times we'll suddenly have to face our deepest struggles. The cage door will shut and we'll find ourselves alone, facing off with an opponent who has bloodied us in the past. What do we do then?

Over the next two chapters I want to show you two strategies that can greatly reduce temptation's power and allow us to avoid its punches.

Both strategies can be illustrated by picturing a river. Think of tempting thoughts as the rushing water pushing us onward in a particular directon. Our first strategy involves asking these questions: *What lies downstream? If I were to follow this flow of thought, where would it ultimately lead?*

The second strategy involves peering upstream. *If these thoughts arrive in my life with the force of raging rapids, where does that power come from? What gives this flow of thought such power in my life?*

In this chapter we'll start by paddling downstream, then turn our eyes upstream in the following one.

TRIALS TRIGGER TEMPTATION

In his letter to his community, James prepared believers for the inevitability of trials. Difficult circumstances would arise for each one of them. He instructed them to *rejoice* in the midst of their suffering, because pain had the potential to build perseverance. And, if they responded to pain with humility, it could even grant wisdom.

But do you know what James addressed next? The inevitability of temptations. The sequence of his argument was intentional, so there is a principle for us here: every trial brings a temptation.

Whenever anything unpleasant happens in our lives, a voice offering sweet release will begin to whisper. We can't avoid it. That voice will give us options of how to respond, many of which will be inappropriate. If these options were to show up on a quiz about morality, you would mark them as immoral or poor choices. Yet in the moment they will feel justified, appropriate, even good.

A coworker constantly gets on your nerves. In a moment of irritation, you may feel the inclination to punch them or cuss them out. Or maybe you'd lean toward a less violent option and want to roll your eyes when they speak, criticize them as soon as their back is turned, or discredit their ideas with comments like, "What you said sounds like something Hitler would say."

Financial pressures will mount and a voice inside will invite you to drown those sorrows in alcohol, or seek solace in the distracting glow of your nearest screen.

The ache of loneliness will become so unbearable that you'll seek out the arms of a stranger so you can feel good for at least one night.

Whenever any difficulty enters your life, a voice in your mind will offer ways to alleviate the attendant discomfort. This voice will be particularly loud and persuasive if you are tired, stressed, or feeling entitled. People in recovery circles often use the acronym HALT to remind themselves to beware whenever they are Hungry, Angry, Lonely, or Tired. These are times when the voice promising sweet release begins to whisper.

Temptations offer to alleviate unease. Discomfort drives desires. We want to change how we feel, to alter our mood, to experience something pleasant, not painful. That's how difficult circumstances can drive us to make damaging decisions. Every trial carries with it temptation—we must be aware and expect it. Much of what will define our lives is not what happens to us but *how we respond* to what happens to us.

James offered two mental tactics to greatly reduce the seductive power of temptation. We will analyze the first in this chapter and the second in the next one. Now we will peer downstream to see where the action leads. *If I engage in this activity now, what will the results be later in my life?*

DESTRUCTION DOWNSTREAM

James stated, "Each person is tempted when he is lured and enticed by his own desire. Then desire when it has conceived gives birth to sin, and sin when it is fully grown brings forth death" (James 1:14–15).

Scripture calls us to consider what the implications of an activity will be *before* we engage in it. This is not a way of thinking that the voice of temptation promotes. When temptation gets in your face, it tries to fill your entire view. It whispers, *I am the only option out there. You have to respond like this!* In your lust you have to click on that image. In your anger you have to punch that guy. In your hurt you have to go to that food or drink or pill or relationship again to block out the pain. It thinks only of the immediate relief. Scripture challenges us to develop the discipline of pushing the temptation aside for a moment and peering downstream. *If I make this decision here, what will the result be? Is that a result I want?*

Alcoholics refer to this discipline as "thinking through the drink." An alcoholic will hear the voice whisper to take a drink. *It'll be just one. Just a sip,* the voice will say. *What harm will a sip do? You're an adult. You can handle it.*

In that moment the tempted person has to develop the mental discipline to say, *No. I know where that leads. One sip will lead to another, then another, and another . . . and then to a host of decisions I will not feel good about tomorrow.*

When James argued this point, he didn't use "rafting downstream" imagery or an illustration about alcohol. Instead, he used sexual imagery: desire lures and entices, then conceives and gives birth.

James's language is reminiscent of a famous Proverbs passage where a father warns his son of a temptress. She will whisper seductive words and promise that the son will not get caught, but ultimately she'll lead the son to destruction.

> With much seductive speech she persuades him;
>> with her smooth talk she compels him.
> All at once he follows her,
>> as an ox goes to the slaughter,
> or as a stag is caught fast
>> till an arrow pierces its liver;
> as a bird rushes into a snare;
>> he does not know that it will cost him his life. . . .
> Her house is the way to Sheol,
>> going down to the chambers of death. (7:21–23, 27)

Temptation does not invite you to do things you find distasteful. It whispers sweetness. It allures with promises of good things. But again and again the writer of Proverbs warned that temptation's honeyed words would turn to poison. Her perfumed bed would become a tomb.

James was even more graphic. He said desire will seduce you. And when you consummate that desire, when you abandon your defenses and unite your will with desire's propositions, she'll get pregnant and have a baby called sin. You brought a little evil into the world, a rebellion against the Author of life. Maybe that thought doesn't bother you too much. But keep looking down the road. When that baby is fully grown, she'll give birth as well, and what she'll bring forth will be death.

These are the scriptural words associated with the downstream destination of temptation: *slaughter, snare, chambers of death.* It's no wonder our Father God wants us to take a beat and look ahead.

Now, keep in mind that having tempting thoughts is not a sin.

But when you enact your will toward that tempting thought—that is a sin. That is your choice.

We don't get to choose our propensities, but we do get to choose our activities.

Biblical scholar Douglas Moo once stated, "Christian maturity is not indicated by the infrequency of temptation but by the infrequency of succumbing to temptation."[1]

A SOLEMN WARNING

One of my pastor friends has a prayer closet in his office. He has filled the room with books, a kneeling bench, and a whiteboard on which he can write the prayer requests of his people. It's all pretty much what you would expect to see in a prayer closet, except for something surprising surrounding the doorway: a series of newspaper clippings with headlines broadcasting the moral failures of prominent pastors.

Why would my friend put those there? Was it some sort of unhealthy fascination? I discovered the answer in a note he wrote in the margin of the most prominent article. It featured a photo of a pastor in his car surrounded by reporters. He had been caught using drugs and sleeping with prostitutes, and the article was from the early days of media coverage when he was still denying allegations. With a big grin and wide hand gestures, the pastor appeared to be spinning the story to his advantage. The pastor's wife was sitting in the passenger seat of the car, and my friend had circled her. Next to her face, he wrote the haunting words, *Look at her eyes.*

She was not looking at her husband or the throng of reporters. She was gazing forward, appearing to look at something a thousand yards away, or at nothing at all. There was a dead expression on her

WE DON'T CHOOSE OUR PROPENSITIES, BUT WE DO CHOOSE OUR ACTIVITIES.

face. Not a hint of joy. No attempt to play along with her husband's narrative. The damage had been done and she knew it. Her face told the real story of heartbreak and betrayal.

Why did my friend write this? It was not for anyone's benefit but his own. It was not gleeful gloating. It was a solemn warning. He knew, as many pastors do, that pastoral work can be emotionally taxing, and in moments of weariness the voice of entitlement can begin to speak. The twin streams of emptiness and entitlement can mingle to create a current that carries pastors downstream into sexual misconduct. Some do it through pornography, others exploit another person in a more direct fashion. Either way, the stream is real and, given enough discomfort, the desire will whisper.

My friend posted this picture as a warning to himself. The message was, *If that voice offering sweet release ever begins to sound like it is making sense, remember this moment. Think about the damage to your wife. Think about the pain it will cause your children. Think about the hurt it will lodge deep into the hearts of people who rely on you. Peer at these faces showing shame, embarrassment, and deep regret, at men who used their power to indulge illicit pleasure. Peer downstream. Sin looks far less sexy in the cold light of day.*

My friend had given himself a visual depiction of the warning against adultery in Proverbs: "The lips of a forbidden woman drip honey, and her speech is smoother than oil, but in the end she is bitter as wormwood, sharp as a two-edged sword" (5:3–4).

LOOK AHEAD AND BREAK THE SPELL

In his autobiography, Johnny Cash recalled his first experience with mood-altering drugs: "I thought, *Boy, this is really something. This is the greatest thing in the world, to make you feel so good when it was hurting so bad.*"[2] Johnny then carried on a love affair with pills throughout many years of his career. He crashed numerous cars while high, once starting a forest fire that nearly wiped out an endangered species of California condor. By the age of thirty-five, he stood six feet, one and a half inches and weighed less than 155 pounds. The romance was killing him.

"All mood-altering drugs carry a demon called Deception," he wrote. "You think, *If this is so bad, why does it feel so good?* I used to tell myself, *God created this; it's got to be the greatest thing in the world.* But it's like the old saying about the wino: he starts by drinking out of the bottle, and then the bottle starts drinking out of him."[3]

Sin looks good, but she brings forth death.

If you continue to feed your addiction to pornography, do you believe it will not grow? Studies show that those who indulge in this form of seduction consistently report awkwardness in relationships, belief that monogamy is unrealistic, and dissatisfaction with actual sex.[4]

If you continue to give full vent to your rage, do you think there will be no price to pay? How many friendships will be lost, marriages ruined, or children damaged downstream from your anger?

Before you take a ride with temptation, look down the stream to see where it will take you. Or, to use James's imagery: before you jump in bed with a given desire, see what kind of baby you will produce. I promise you, thousands of men and women who have committed adultery would have resisted the romantic impulse of the moment if they had just paused long enough to imagine the devastation their indiscretion would cause later on—a lost career, a ruined reputation, a broken family. Johnny may have been spared years of pain and self-destruction if he had looked ahead and seen what drugs would ultimately do to his body and his relationships.

When you let your mind consider the consequences downstream, it breaks the spell. It shatters the illusion. It shuts down the seduction.

It dispels the lies that say, *You won't get caught. No one will know. It's not harming anyone.* Or, *The bad things that happened to them won't happen to me. I'll make sure of it.*

Maybe you are already beginning to lean on the same coping mechanisms you've seen modeled in your family—and you know they weren't helpful to them. You've seen where it goes. Before you hop in the boat, turn your ear downstream and hear the distant crash of the waterfall. Stop and think carefully. Are you really going to take the route that will leave you dashed upon the same rocks that have shattered so many lives before?

Not all lessons need to be learned the hard way. You're in a position to learn from others' mistakes and your own mistakes.

You get to choose what you'll do.

RHYTHMS OF WAR

1. Write out James 1:12–15 in your journal.
2. Think of a moment in your life when a trial made a temptation look attractive.
3. Recall a failure in your past. Do you believe that considering the outcome of that decision would have helped you resist the first impulse?

CHAPTER 7

LOOK UPSTREAM

Something was making the children of Bryan, Texas, sick. Residents living near Bryan Municipal Lake noticed that multiple babies were born with severe birth defects. And that wasn't the only clue that something was off. Others discovered that several of the fish in the lake were missing fins or eyes. Turtles grew strange scales that covered their nostrils. After some careful investigation, researchers figured out why: something was wrong with the water.

Studies revealed that the lake water showed concentrations of arsenic twelve times higher than the Environmental Protection Agency's maximum limit for safe drinking water. Elevated levels of arsenic in the human body can lead to vomiting, abdominal pain and, at high enough levels, cancer and death. A critical question remained: How had that water become toxic?

Finally someone had the idea to take a look upstream. They discovered that Bryan Municipal Lake was fed by Fin Feather Lake, which was near Cotton Poisons Inc., a chemical company that created arsenic-based herbicides. Toxic runoff from the factory's retention ponds had been flowing into the lakes below.

Only by paddling upstream did researchers discover the source of the sickness. Only after discovering the cause could they effectively work to resolve the problem.[1]

The same principle applies to our understanding of temptation. To truly grasp why our temptations have such power in our lives, we must paddle upstream and discover the fountain from which they spring. We could spend all our time and energy fighting the symptoms, but we will find substantial healing only if we treat the disease.

John Owen stated, "He that would indeed get the conquest over any sin must consider his temptations to it, and strike at the root; without deliverance from thence, he will not be healed."[2] So if your temptation is a poisonous tree, removing only the poisonous fruit from the branches or the ground won't fix the issue. More fruit will grow in. You have to attack that tree *at its root*.

If you want to defeat an enemy in war, you must cut its supply lines. You have to starve it from its fresh stores of munitions. It is the same with the struggles in our lives. We have to identify what is fueling our struggles internally and disrupt the patterns of temptation.

That starts by looking at what we believe, because what we believe in the deepest parts of us determines what we do. Proverbs 20:5 says, "The purpose in a man's heart is like deep water, but a man of understanding will draw it out." We must become the kind of people who do this. Only at the headwaters of our hearts will we find the source of our temptation's strength.

Let's paddle upstream into our heart's beliefs and motivations.

HEADWATERS REVEAL THE SOURCE

For many of us our addictions are an escape from pain. The wound that causes the pain probably happened long ago and likely went unaddressed. When you received the wound, you also believed a lie. Maybe your parents divorced and, in a moment of pain, a lie crept into your heart: *You are not worth fighting for.*

Maybe it was a moment when you saw your father's disappointment in you—you could see it on his face. Your heart received the message: *You are not enough.*

Or maybe your father was silent when you desperately needed a voice of blessing in your life. The words never came. And with that deep wound came a belief: *You are alone. No one will support you.*

If we are honest, many of us who are workaholics might just find that under our "ambition" and "discipline" is a sad little kid who just wanted their dad's approval. The lie *You are not accepted or loved* is still embedded in our hearts, and no amount of money or success can heal our wound.

Now, looking at your deep wounds and your responses to them can leave you swimming in shame. That shame can make you want to run away from all of it—to avoid it, deny it, or numb it. But ignoring a wound will not heal it. You do not mend a broken leg by pretending it does not exist—that will eventually cause problems for your entire body! You must face the injury. You must understand it so you can heal it. And when you are really ready to take it seriously, you must go all the way back to the original wound. The deepest cut.

After James explained how temptation worked, he said, "Do not be deceived, my beloved brothers" (1:16). There's another key about how temptation works here. Our mind believes something that is not true, and that distortion of truth disorders our affections. Then we begin to willfully choose to go to the wrong places for answers or relief or comfort. *Temptation begins with deception.*

Notice the nature of the deception. James stated, "Do not be deceived. . . . Every good gift and every perfect gift is from above, coming down from the Father of lights, with whom there is no variation or shadow due to change" (vv. 16–17). He didn't begin to enumerate a laundry list of deceptions that believers might fall for—like cheating is no big deal, or lying is life-enhancing, or adultery is fun. He didn't look at the actions they might take downstream. He instead looked up to the headwaters to identify the source of their pain, which was stemming from their relationship with God.

Our deepest problems are not rooted in procrastination or workaholism, lust or pride, fear or resentment, or even father wounds or family trauma. The deepest source of our sickness is a failure to understand something fundamental about the nature of our God. We often fail to see God as a Father who gives good gifts to his children. We begin to doubt that he will be someone we can count on. We start to think he will shift on us or suddenly change, or stop being gracious or trustworthy or good.

We believe the lie that launches a million sins—the lie that God is not a good Father who will take care of us.

THE GARDEN DECEPTION DISASTER

We see this so clearly in the garden of Eden. When the serpent first approached Eve, he did not come with some insane proposition, like, "Hey, let's smoke crack and kill Adam!" She would have flatly refused. How did he begin the conversation?

He asked her, "Did God really say, 'You must not eat from any tree in the garden'?" (Genesis 3:1 NIV).

The serpent started the conversation with theology. But look at how he did it: the name he used for God was the Hebrew word *Elohim*, which highlights his power. It's translated as "God"—which is certainly not a bad way to refer to God! Throughout Genesis 2, however, God is referred to as *Yahweh Elohim*, or "the LORD God" (*twelve times*, in fact). Yahweh is his covenantal name, the special name he wanted his people to call him so they'd remember he loved them and had bound himself to them.

So the Enemy said, "Let's talk theology," and then left out God's covenantal name. It was a small shift, but not an insignificant one. It is easier to transgress the laws of a distant deity than violate a relationship with the One who loves you intimately.

Think about the seasons in life when you made your worst integrity-compromising decisions. If you trace it back, I would imagine they were seasons when you felt the most relational distance from God. If you cool the fires of your affection for God, you will go to find warmth somewhere else.

Let's look back at the nature of Satan's question. He in essence said, "Eve, it seems like God has put some limitations on you. You can't eat from any tree you want, can you? He's holding out on you. Your religious convictions seem to be costing you an intriguing experience. Am I right, Eve?"

Eve responded by repeating God's commands, but she misquoted him in three ways.

First, the original language shows us that God had said, "Eat, eat!" (2:16). In Hebrew, if you want to emphasize a word, you repeat it. And God, in his first command to the young couple, doubled up the word *eat*. It was a command to discover and enjoy all he had made! When Eve recited it, though, she said it only once: "We may eat" (3:2). She undervalued God's privileges. He sounded way less generous and way less fun.

Next, Eve said they could not eat from the tree in the middle of the garden, or touch it (v. 3). But God did not say they could not touch it. They could tie a swing on it or build a tree house in it. They just couldn't *eat* the fruit. She added to God's prohibitions. In doing so she made God more of a killjoy than he ever made himself out to be.

Finally, Eve told the serpent, "God said, 'You shall not eat . . . lest you die" (v. 3). This was wrong as well. According to the Hebrew, God had said, "Die, die." He doubled this word as well. Literally he said, "Dying you will die." You will lose spiritual life and physical life. Here, Eve weakened the strength of God's penalty.

Do you see how Eve's report made God sound? God was less personal. He was less generous and more restrictive. And he was less majestic. Satan intentionally weakened her view of God's beauty and severity. Then, and only then, did he press his advantage.

The temptation will not look beautiful unless God looks less lovely first.

Satan convinced Eve that to truly experience life she must rebel against the Author of life. No more trusting God to tell her what is best; she must become the arbiter of what is truly good and evil. That was the true temptation of the tree. It was not just the experience of knowing good and evil; it was an attempt to grab the power of becoming the one who gets to decide what is good and evil.

Eve took matters into her own hands. Why? Because she believed God's hands were not trustworthy. This is the deception under the rebellion. It was never about fruit. It was about believing, *God is not worthy to trust with my desires because he won't take good care of me.* And when Eve believed that, she took the fruit, and a tsunami of sin and death broke into the world.

Do you see it? *Every temptation ends in destruction and begins with deception.*

LIES ABOUT OUR FATHER
AND OUR SONSHIP

This is the deception James warned believers about. We have to watch out for the lie that every good and perfect gift does *not* come down from our Father above. We must resist any message saying that he shifts and changes, that he is unreliable and untrustworthy, or that he won't take care of us. We must not believe his counsel is unsound, his warnings are frivolous, or his ways will keep us from a fulfilling life. We've got to push back against anything that suggests his heart is not good.

Let's say you decided to hate me. On your list of goals for the upcoming year you include, "Destroy Ben Stuart!" Let me tell you how to do it. I'll go ahead and reveal to you the worst possible thing you could do to me: approach one of my three elementary school–age children, strike up a conversation with them, and work to convince them that I do not care about them. Tell them they don't measure up to my standards. Look them in the eye and tell them I am endlessly disappointed in them, that I don't love them or like them, and that they're a burden, hassle, and disappointment to me. Then convince them that the best thing to do would be to run away. Find love in the arms of some other father figure. Find shelter somewhere on the streets. Tell them not to look to me to feed, clothe, house, love, teach, or guide them. Go anywhere else to find love and truth and wisdom. The most evil thing you could do to me would be driving a wedge between my precious kids and me.

Do not miss this, friend: this is what the Enemy does to you.

In the same passage where John told believers that Jesus came to destroy the works of the devil, he also said, "See what kind of love the

Father has given to us, that we should be called children of God; and so we are" (1 John 3:1).

The Enemy's lies are aimed at your sonship. Your identity determines your activity, and if you believe you are the unloved, unlovable, discarded son, then you will wander in foreign lands looking to fill that void or numb that ache. But when Jesus makes war with the devil, it is a war to convince you of a vital truth: You are a child of God. And he is a loving Father.

James presented evidence to bolster his argument that God is a good Father. He declared, "Of his own will he brought us forth by the word of truth, that we should be a kind of firstfruits of his creatures" (1:18).

He brought you forth—and it was prompted not by your work, but by his will. He brought you forth—not because of your performance, but because of his desire and love for you. God made you alive by means of the truth. Remember this when the lies begin to speak. *My Father sent for me. My Jesus died for me. That's what is true.*

Do you want to destroy the work of the devil in your life? Do you want to overcome the pull of the world? This is the field of battle. See and believe. Behold what manner of love the Father has given unto us, that we would be called the sons of God. And. So. We. Are.

HOW HE LOVES US

I would like to make a confession to you: I disliked the song "How He Loves Us" for years. I know this is not a popular sentiment in Christian circles. I would often instinctively roll my eyes when a worship band started the first few notes of the song and the crowd cheered in anticipation. Then I began to question that impulse. *Why do I hate this song? Is it the lyrics, or the melody?* That wasn't it. What was it?

Finally, I realized: *It's because I don't believe it.* The song invited us to say over and over again how much God loved us, and when I said it out loud, a part of me would become angry—because I just didn't believe it.

At a very deep place inside of me, I believed fathers didn't care about their kids. I had so much anger in me that, when I rowed upstream, I discovered this belief began when I was around eight years old. My dad did not spend much time with me. I always felt like I disappointed him. My mind could easily and vividly recall a memory of him turning his back on me in embarrassment when I failed to field a ball during a baseball game. I often saw in my mind's eye the photo of Parents Day for the football team when my dad didn't show up for my game. I remember every sight, sound, and smell from the moments my parents sat me down and told me they were getting a divorce.

I felt unloved and unlovable.

Like many of us, I ascribed the feelings I associated with my earthly father to my heavenly Father. He had let all this happen, after all. I deeply believed he didn't care. If I was ever going to feel love, or at least escape from the pain, then I would have to go elsewhere. Porn was waiting there for me at age nine. Workaholism, motivated by desperation for approval, kick-started around age twelve.

Fast-forward to my adult years, when I was thirty-five and our daughter Hannah was a newborn. She woke up every few hours throughout the night, and I always took the early morning shift with her. As the sun slowly rose, I would sit on the couch in silence just holding this little girl, a life that was literally the product of the love of her parents. I would run my fingers across her tiny feet and soft cheeks and watch as her little fingers curled instinctively around one of mine. I marveled at her.

One morning as we did this, I felt a sudden, deep pain in my chest.

It felt as though my heart would explode. What was happening? Was it a heart attack? A lung collapsing? Then I realized—no, this was love! This enormous exploding feeling in my chest was love for my baby girl, and it astounded me. This child had done nothing for me. She hadn't complimented my sermons. She hadn't cleaned up around the house or pitched in to pay rent. She had been nothing but inconvenience and need. Hunger surrounded by noise. But, entirely independent of her activities, I felt a deep and profound love for her that I could not begin to express. I wished there was a way I could place into that tiny brain of hers an understanding of the love that coursed through her father's heart.

Then I felt that sweet and deep, comforting and convicting voice of God speak into that silence, "Ben, do you think you are a more loving father than I am?"

And I wept.

There on that couch I had to repent of an unbiblically low view of the love of God. I had let pain congeal into anger and used anger as a shield against pain. Anger at God. Anger at my dad. I had preserved unfair assumptions about them both based on heavily interpreted images from my childhood and amended out any evidence to the contrary. I had to repent embracing the lie that I was unloved.

Patrick Carnes, one of the leading voices on sexual addiction in America, once explained that addiction stems from feeling unloved and unlovable. Addiction is an intimacy disorder.[3] I believe this is why the Enemy works so tirelessly to unravel healthy fatherhood in the world. If he can drive a wedge between children and the love of their fathers, he can more easily drive a wedge between the children of God and their rest in the inexhaustible love of their heavenly Father.

I will tell you this though: if you dismantle a false belief about God's character, then you will defuse a bomb that would have otherwise sent untold shrapnel into your spiritual life. When I repented of that low view of God's love, I could feel the power source of my addictions suffer a catastrophic blow. The lie that I was unloved had been like a motor driving my actions—my cycle of striving for approval and then retreating to addictive behaviors. But when I opened up my heart to God in faith and humility, I realized he could overpower any lie or cycle of behaviors I'd felt stuck with for years. I could believe and sing about his overwhelming, inexhaustible love. I could let it usher in healing in my relationship with my dad and change the way I viewed myself. I could let it settle into my soul and give me true rest.

Addiction loses its strength when the affection of God is embraced.

THE EMPOWERING PLEASURE
OF THE FATHER

This was the great weapon Jesus wielded against Satan in his earthly ministry. Remember how we discussed earlier that he began his earthly campaign in the baptismal waters with John the Baptist? As he entered the water, a voice from heaven declared, "This is my beloved Son, with whom I am well pleased" (Matthew 3:17). The affection of God on full display.

This happened before Jesus had done a single thing in his ministry. No miracles performed. No sick people healed. Not a single sermon preached.

God's loving identification with his children does not wait upon our actions. His love flies first.

Armed with the knowledge of God's affection for him, Jesus headed into the desert to face off with Satan. The devil tempted him to distrust God's plans for provision, and Jesus refused. God would feed him. Satan offered him power without persecution, and Jesus dismissed him again.

The Enemy's propaganda loses power in the light of God's promises.

Later on at the midpoint of his ministry, when Jesus began his trek toward Jerusalem, the heavens opened again. God again pronounced, "This is my beloved Son, with whom I am well pleased" (Matthew 17:5). Armed with that love, Jesus could rebuff Satan's offer to refuse the cross. Jesus could endure trials and refuse temptations because he won the battle of belief. He knew he was a loved Son, and his actions flowed from his Father's unfettered acceptance.

I once heard pastor Louie Giglio say it this way: "It was the pleasure of God that led Jesus through the pressure of the desert." This is true for us as well.

The early church practiced baptism in a way that focused on this. They led new converts to embrace God's affection for them by telling them to picture the moment of Jesus' baptism during their own. They imagined Jesus standing in the water with them. They imagined the Spirit of God arriving to fill them. And they imagined the voice of their Father in heaven saying over them, "This is my child, with whom I am well pleased." They went on to find great joy even in seasons of persecution, because they'd gripped the grace of their loving heavenly Father.

I promise you, friend, the pleasure of your Father will empower you to face the problems of today.

John Owen said that "every act of sin is a fruit of being weary of God."[4] The inverse is true too. Every refusal of temptation draws its strength from a delight in God.

Here lies our most potent weapon against temptation: the best defense is a good offense.

EVERY REFUSAL OF TEMPTATION DRAWS ITS STRENGTH FROM A DELIGHT IN GOD.

Remember that story about when Donna and I bought our first home and the yard was covered with weeds? We consulted an expert on lawn and turf management (we were serious!). He counseled us to go ahead and pull the large, invasive weeds but not to try to pull every single weed. There were millions. He said there was a better strategy: feed the grass. Keep mowing and seeding and nurturing the little bit of grass that existed in the midst of our massive weed patch. He explained that if we prioritized tending to the healthy grass, it would, in time, overpower this ocean of weeds. The best way to defeat the weeds was to feed the grass.

It is the same with our affections. The best way to overpower our broken and sad desires is to invest in our beautiful and sanctified ones.

The best defense against adultery is a strong, thriving marriage.

The best guard against toxic and codependent relationships is involvement in healthy, restorative community.

And the best approach to dislodging a persistent affection from the human heart is inviting the expulsive power of a new one.

EXPULSIVE POWER OF A
NEW AFFECTION

This was nineteenth-century minister Thomas Chalmers's glorious observation in his classic sermon, "The Expulsive Power of a New Affection." Tim Keller summarized Chalmers's words like this: "The only way to dispossess the heart of an old affection is by the expulsive power of a new one. . . . It is not enough to hold to the world the mirror of its own imperfections. It is not enough to come forth with a demonstration of the evanescent character of your enjoyments . . . to speak to the conscience . . . of its follies. . . . Rather, try every legitimate method of finding access to your hearts for the love of Him who is greater than the world."⁵

We can't just focus on the negativity of our broken desires. We also need to let ourselves be swept up by the beauty of our sanctified ones.

Shakespeare put this very idea on display. How did Romeo get rid of Rosaline? Do you even remember Rosaline? At the outset of Shakespeare's most famous play, Romeo pines away incessantly for his beloved Rosaline. Finally, in frustration, Benvolio tells him he's going to take Romeo to a party where there would be a hundred girls hotter than Rosaline (that's a rough translation, but go look at it, it's there).

And what was Romeo's response? "The all-seeing sun ne'er saw her match since first the world begun."⁶ Whoa. Apparently, there was no one in existence hotter than Rosaline.

He went to the party anyway. He saw Juliet, and before he knew it, he was sneaking into her yard and looking at her on her balcony, exclaiming, "But soft, what light through yonder window breaks? It is the east, and Juliet is the sun! Arise, fair sun, and kill the envious moon, who is already sick and pale with grief that thou her maid art far more fair than she."⁷

Rosaline who?

It is the same with you, friend! Any unhealthy thing that is holding your attention today can be overwhelmed with something better. Your addictions lose their allure in the light of God's affections.

He is the fountain of living water and the water that wells up to eternal life (Jeremiah 2:12–13; John 4:13–14)! In his presence is fullness of joy! In his right hand are pleasures forevermore (Psalm 16:11). So we are meant to follow the command in Psalm 37:4: "Delight yourself in the LORD."

This is how the great Saint Augustine found deliverance from his addictions to glory and sex. He knew that to embrace Jesus meant to leave his sexual promiscuity behind, and he was terrified to let go of such a deeply entrenched source of comfort in his life. As he wrestled with God, he took up his copy of the Scriptures and read: "Put on the Lord Jesus Christ, and make no provision for the flesh, to gratify its desires" (Romans 13:14).

He chose to abandon one set of activities—and then he embraced another.

Augustine wrote, "How sweet all at once it was for me to be rid of those fruitless joys which I had once feared to lose. . . . You drove them from me, You who are the true, the sovereign joy. You drove them from me and took their place, You who are sweeter than all pleasure."[8]

We release one treasure so we can grip a better and abiding one.

The best way to rise up out of the dust is to set your mind on the things that are above and to let them reach down into the deepest parts of you.

Get honest about what you really believe. See the wounds and the lies. Welcome in the healing, empowering truth. Open yourself up to your Father's affection and his love that flies first—before you ever somehow prove yourself lovable. Go ahead and get swept up in the one who is "sweeter than all pleasure" and can give you true joy.

RHYTHMS OF WAR

1. Take a moment to write out James 1:16–18 in your journal.
2. Do you believe God is a good Father? If so, how? If not, why?
3. Make a list of the good gifts that he has given you.

PART 3

REST

CHAPTER 8

THE PROPER PURSUIT

On sunny days in my college years, lots of girls would go to a park to study and lie out. Naturally young men also would go, to be around the girls. Over time a strategy developed: Guys would bring the cutest dogs they could find to the park. Girls would ask to pet this assortment of adorable pets, and the guys would have their chance at sparking a conversation.

I had a roommate at the time who wanted to be one of those guys. Because he wanted to be with one of those girls. So he needed one of those dogs.

Now, my friend could barely feed and clothe himself. No way was it a good idea to bring a dog into his chaotic life. Whenever he talked about getting a dog, my buddies and I strongly discouraged it. But he had a vision, and he was undeterred. One day, sure enough, he brought home a gorgeous animal.

I say *animal* because it turned out she was three-quarters

wolf—which I didn't know was a thing, but it is (pretty sure it's not a legal thing, by the way). She was beautiful.

I will never forget the first sunny day of that semester. My roommate bounded into the living room carrying a leash and a tennis ball. He smiled at us and announced, "Time to go to the park!" I watched as he and the wolf skipped out the front door, off to fulfill his destiny. Not long afterward the wolf trotted happily back into the living room. My roommate stumbled in after her and collapsed onto the couch.

"What happened?" I asked.

He proceeded to tell me the story of what transpired at the park.

When he arrived at the fields filled with young women lying on blankets reading and chatting, he unleashed the wolf. He tossed the tennis ball lazily past the girls and it rolled into a nearby bush. From behind him he heard a voice say, "Beautiful dog you have there." It was an older man who was an avid dog lover. Not really the attention my friend was looking for. But he paused to visit with the man about breeding and whatnot. Suddenly their conversation was interrupted by the sounds of young women screaming.

My friend turned around to face the field of dreams and immediately saw the cause of the cries of terror. His wolf was slowly trotting back toward him through the sea of girls, carrying something. It wasn't the tennis ball he had thrown. Nope, she was carrying a cute, fuzzy bunny. That was bleeding.

Apparently the wolf had discovered a new game to play. She'd throw the wounded bunny into the air, and as it would thud to the earth and struggle to escape, she'd pounce and tear into it.

This once-tranquil scene was now filled with crying girls burying their faces in one another's arms to shield their eyes from the horror playing out before them. My friend had to run out there in the middle of the girls, finish off the rabbit, pick up the wolf, and run as quickly as possible back to his car.

Needless to say, this was a far cry from his expectations for the afternoon. Shortly thereafter he gave the wolf away to a lovely family of four.

Now, let me ask you a question. What went wrong? The answer is simple: my friend brought a wolf to the park! This creature looked like a dog—she had fur, four legs, and a tail. But she was not a dog. She was a wild, unpredictably violent animal. Instead of boosting my friend's social image, she was a force of destruction. He expected her to do something she was not designed to do, to meet a need she couldn't meet. And at the moment he needed her, she not only failed him, she was destructive.

Now, why do I tell you this? Because we're about to explore various strategies for pursuing a truly spiritual life, and I want to issue a word of caution: There is a version of spirituality that looks a lot like the real thing, but it is not. If we choose it, it will not only fail us; it will be destructive.

SPIRITUALITY THAT DOES MORE HARM THAN GOOD

When I ask people to describe what it means to be *spiritual* or *godly* or *religious*, they often begin to make a list of things a good spiritual person does and does not do. Spiritual people attend religious services, pray, meditate, read Scripture, and serve. They also avoid going to certain places, saying certain things, and doing particular acts. Without realizing it, these people have defined spirituality as adhering to a list of dos and don'ts.

You may have experienced this form of spirituality. Maybe you were forced to obey a list like this as a kid. Or maybe you made a resolution at some point in your life to obey some list of religious directives because you felt like you needed a spiritual dimension to your life. But there is a problem with this whole way of framing the conversation. This version of spirituality virtually guarantees one of two outcomes.

First, you will eventually get frustrated and ditch the list. Maybe you grew up under strict religious parents and in college you cast off your repressive restraints. Or maybe you joined a church out of a sincere desire to grow spiritually, but you just couldn't seem to live up to the standard, and after a while you got tired of feeling like a failure. So you quit. Perhaps you tried on some kind of spiritual observance or a book of rules for life, but your friends who didn't bind themselves to any rules seemed to be having more fun. The scenarios abound here, but the short story is, the list of dos and don'ts got frustrating. So you eventually just forgot the whole thing.

Or second, and what I believe is far more dangerous, you've kept the list perfectly. You've obeyed all the rules. You've excelled at all the expectations. Now you look around at all the pathetic people who can't seem to get it together and you judge them. You pity them for their weakness, or you disdain them for their lack of discipline. You've been nurturing a smug self-righteousness because you are capable of something lesser mortals are not. And in your arrogance your heart has grown very cold.

Whether you are running from the rules or obsessing over them, here is the point: Neither of these things is Christianity. Neither is what God wants from you or for you.

When I took on the role of husband, there were certain responsibilities that came with that new role. You could make a list of what good husbands do. They (1) take out the trash, (2) put gas in the car, and (3) defend the family when wild animals attack. (That last one doesn't come up much, but all husbands know what their job will be if it ever occurs.)

Let me tell you something though. When Donna and I fell in love, got married, and left our wedding, we did not race back to the hotel and make a list of responsibilities. No, we went to Jamaica! We hiked in Seattle and swam in the ocean in Hawaii! When we moved into our new apartment together, we went on walks. We went to the movies. We spent hours talking, sometimes laughing, sometimes crying. We loved each other and enjoyed each other.

Now, as we grew in our love together, I began to do things that would be on a list if we had made a list. I took out the trash, because I didn't want my girl carrying out the garbage. I put gas in the car because I found joy in serving her. And you had better believe I'd sacrifice myself to defend her in the case of any animal attack!

But do you see the difference? One version is following a list, while the other is loving a person. One is obeying the rules, the other is cultivating the relationship. One is counterfeit—though in the day-to-day, it can look like the real thing. I could accomplish every task on a husband to-do list and still have a soulless, lifeless marriage. The other naturally does all of these activities and sees them as a means to an end, not the end in itself. They are actions undertaken to cultivate intimacy, not to fulfill some standard of morality. Do you see the difference? This is no small shift in thinking.

True spirituality is not adherence to a list of rules or activities; it is investment in the greatest of all relationships. While this cultivation involves doing activities, those activities are a means, not an end. And that makes all the difference.

LISTIANITY VS. INTIMACY

I am not a huge fan of the term *spiritual disciplines*. It is not at all wrong to use this language, but my concern is that it opens the door for us to make discipline the end and not the means. We may be simply aiming to become a more disciplined person, which is in the realm of fitness or self-improvement. The metric of success is our ability to set goals and accomplish tasks and become a more organized person.

But that is not spirituality.

True spirituality is more dynamic than that because it is a relationship with a Being, the greatest of all beings. So there are activities—or disciplines, if you like—involved. But they *build toward something*, just like dates or game nights or road trips bring you closer to the people in your life. True spirituality is not simply the execution of disciplines; it is the cultivation of intimacy.

Here is the crazy thing about the "listianity" version of spirituality: not only does it miss the point of cultivating intimacy with God, it doesn't really work in pulling you back from temptation.

The apostle Paul addressed this issue with the Colossians. He told them: "If with Christ you died to the elemental spirits of the world, why, as if you were still alive in the world, do you submit to regulations—'Do not handle, Do not taste, Do not touch' . . . according to human precepts and teachings? These have indeed an appearance of wisdom in promoting self-made religion and asceticism and severity to the body, but they are of no value in stopping the indulgence of the flesh" (Colossians 2:20–23).

The Colossian believers were dutifully following harsh ascetic practices in the name of pleasing God, but those practices did not prevent them from living a life controlled by their wayward impulses.

No wonder some people believe this type of experience sums up

TRUE SPIRITUALITY IS THE CULTIVATION OF INTIMACY.

true religion—they see others follow a bunch of repressive rules then eventually give up on them. They watch as these frustrated people release the floodgates of their passions, either by publicly renouncing their powerless religion or by privately indulging in the very things they publicly condemned. *Guess religion doesn't work, huh?* the people looking on think. They don't realize they were watching the simple execution of disciplines, not the cultivation of intimacy.

DEVOTION OVER DISCIPLINE

Paul told Timothy, "The goal of our instruction is love from a pure heart, from a good conscience, and from a sincere faith" (1 Timothy 1:5 NASB).

Our target is not discipline, it is devotion. If your study of God's Word or attendance at religious services does not cultivate a deeper love for him in your heart, then you are doing it wrong.

In Paul's pre-apostle life, he was a religious performance junkie. I mean, he was obsessed. He reveled in his titles, status, education, demonstrations of zeal, and conformity to the law. After his life-changing encounter with Jesus, though, his whole world shifted. He said, "Whatever gain I had, I counted as loss for the sake of Christ. Indeed, I count everything as loss because of the surpassing worth of knowing Christ Jesus my Lord. For his sake I have suffered the loss of all things and count them as rubbish, in order that I may gain Christ" (Philippians 3:7–8).

What Paul once so cherished—the accumulation of accolades and accomplishments—he now considered garbage! What did he prize now? Truly knowing Jesus. Intimacy with him.

Not only did Paul say that knowing Christ was his prize, he said it was his ongoing pursuit. "Not that I have already obtained this or am already perfect, but I press on to make it my own, because Christ Jesus has made me his own" (v. 12).

Christ had made Paul his own, chasing him down and laying claim to him. Now Paul's joyful aim in life was to pursue an unrestrained enjoyment of the God who would come for him when he was a self-righteous wreck!

We get to have the same joyful aim in life Paul had. We get to use all manner of activities for the great aim of enjoying the One who gladly gave himself up for us. Any discipline we practice is a way to express and deepen our devotion to the Almighty. Paul called this the mature way to perceive the Christian life. Our pursuit is a Person, not a set of practices.

Paul didn't want believers to lose this aim. He once expressed his concern about it in terms of fear: "I am afraid that as the serpent deceived Eve by his cunning, your thoughts will be led astray from a sincere and pure devotion to Christ" (2 Corinthians 11:3). We must be watchful of this subtle detour the devil might launch into our minds at this point in our journey. The goal is an honest and sincere pursuit of intimacy with the Almighty. Anything less is disappointing and dangerous.

For this reason I prefer the word *devotion*. In Greek the word we translate as *devotion* is the combination of the words *good* and *beside*. This is the aim of the Christian life: to become increasingly *good* at being close *beside* the Lord, to really know and love him.

When Jesus was asked what the greatest commandment was, he said, "Love the Lord your God with all your heart and with all your soul and with all your mind" (Matthew 22:37). The goal of all our endeavors is love. So let's ditch "listianity" and take up true Christianity. Let's be watchful against a soulless religion and stay centered on soul-satisfying relationship.

How do we do this? In the previous section we discussed how the Enemy exploits our wiring and tendencies to derail us from our purpose and destroy our lives. Now here is the good news. The same mind, affections, and will the Enemy manipulates for evil can be harnessed for good. You have the power to use them to pursue what you treasure most.

RESET YOUR MIND TO
CHANGE YOUR MINDSET

However you conceive of spirituality, it is primarily a *battle of the mind*. What you think about is what you will care about, and what you care about, you will chase. That's why Paul told the Colossians, "Set your mind on things that are above" (3:2). If you want to change your mindset, you need to change what you set your mind upon. Our actions are chosen based on the options presented.

A changed life begins with a changed mind.

When Paul called the Romans to no longer be "conformed to this world," he presented the means of renovation: "Be transformed by the renewal of your mind" (Romans 12:2). He understood that "to set the mind on the flesh is death, but to set the mind on the Spirit is life and peace" (8:6).

When he told the Ephesians, "Put off your old self," he also said, "Be renewed in the spirit of your minds" (Ephesians 4:22–23).

When he called the Philippians to abandon an inferior, rules-based version of spirituality, he challenged them, "Whatever is true, whatever is honorable, whatever is just, whatever is pure, whatever is lovely, whatever is commendable, if there is any excellence, if there is anything worthy of praise, think about these things" (Philippians 4:8).

The first step we take, the step championed over and over again in the Scriptures, is to load our mind with thoughts of God.

The key is to remember we're not talking about a mere mental exercise. As we saw earlier: "The goal of our instruction is love from a pure heart, from a good conscience, and from a sincere faith" (1 Timothy 1:5 NASB).

In Jonathan Edwards's expansive treatise on the nature of spirituality, he concluded, "True religion consists in holy affections."[1] *Knowledge of God serves as the fuel for the fires of our affections for him.*

When I first met Donna, I was immediately attracted to her. I felt a stirring for her in my heart. What did that internal impulse drive me to do? To talk to her. To go to dinner with her. To call her on the phone and to read the notes she wrote me. What was I doing? What all of us do—feeding the fires of our passions with information. I wanted to know her more because love seeks knowledge of the beloved.

We load our minds with thoughts of God to stir our hearts with a passion for God, which propels us to live lives that honor and enjoy God. The more we see him, the more we become like him. The more we become like him, the more we fulfill our created intent as image bearers in the world.

Paul explained to the Corinthians, "We all, with unveiled face, beholding the glory of the Lord, are being transformed into the same image from one degree of glory to another" (2 Corinthians 3:18). *Beholding becomes transforming.* When we look more and more like him, we begin to take up our God-given calling that we misplaced long ago.

So go behold him.

Go seek the knowledge of your Beloved.

Find ways to cultivate intimacy with the Almighty and deepen your devotion to him.

Harness all the means at your disposal to build a life where you flourish under him and enjoy him.

RHYTHMS OF REST

1. Have you seen in yourself a propensity to reduce spirituality to a list of rules or activities? If so, what does that look like in your life?
2. Think about your closest relationships. What activities do you naturally do to deepen and strengthen those bonds?
3. Take a moment and talk to God about the concept of cultivating intimacy with him. Process with him what fears or questions you may have. Ask him to give you a vision of what activities you may want to introduce to your life to deepen your devotion to him.

| ' | ' ' ' | ' ' ' ' | ' ' ' ' | ' ' ' ' | ' ' ' ' | ' ' ' ' | ' ' ' ' | ' ' ' ' | ' ' ' ' | ' ' ' ' | ' ' ' ' | ' ' ' ' | ' ' ' ' | ' ' ' ' | ' ' ' ' |

1   2   3   4   5   6   7   8   (9)   10   11   12   13   14   15

CHAPTER 9

FROM ANXIETY TO INTIMACY

While showering one day in college, I suddenly felt a sharp pain in my chest. As the pressure continued to mount, it became difficult to breathe. My mind began to race. *Why is this happening? Was it the barbecue?* I had been eating off a plate of leftover barbecue for a week and a half. *Is the barbecue killing me?* I began to pray, *Lord, please don't let me go out like this!*

What a stupid way to die! I thought. I pictured people at the funeral: "How did this happen?" one would whisper. "Barbecue," another would answer. "He kept eating leftovers far beyond a reasonable expiration date."

I managed to survive the shower. But for the next several days it hurt to breathe. Finally all the fear and uncertainty drove me to make an appointment with my doctor. He peppered me with questions.

"Do you drink?"

"No."

"Do you smoke?"

"No."

"Are you stressed?"

Pause . . . "No?"

He heard my hesitation. I felt the need to expound.

"I'm concerned about finals coming up, and the multiple organizations I'm a leader in, and what major to choose, and how I'm going to pay for school, and how to afford rent this month, and whether the girl I'm dating is 'the one,' and if I'm emotionally ready for commitment, and what is emotionally wrong with me as a human, and what I'm going to do with the rest of my life . . ."

"Whoa, whoa, whoa," he interrupted. "That's your problem. You're stressed. You need to calm down."

As I left his office, I paused for a moment to ponder my predicament. I was amazed at the idea that something completely intangible, like the experience of stress, could have such profound physical implications. I learned that day to respect the power of anxiety.

Some of you know what I'm talking about. You may not have had heart problems or a fear that barbecue was killing you, but you've had the sleepless nights, the racing thoughts, the shallow breathing. You have wondered, *How am I going to get this done? When am I going to figure that out? How is this situation going to play out? What are they going to think?* You know what it is to be plagued by stress.

Why mention this in a chapter that's meant to be about cultivating intimacy with God? We begin here because, if we're honest, this is where many of us begin our days. We live in a culture of stress.

DANGERS OF ANXIETY

Over the last several years multiple reports have warned about the soaring levels of stress and anxiety, particularly among young people.

Something about the constant barrage of information, observation, and analysis of life through social media has been toxic to the human spirit. For many of us our problems are not our greatest problem; our *anxiety about* our problems is.

Jesus said, "Do not be anxious, saying, 'What shall we eat?' or 'What shall we drink?' or 'What shall we wear?' . . . But seek first the kingdom of God and his righteousness, and all these things will be added to you" (Matthew 6:31, 33). Notice that he contrasted dwelling in anxiety with seeking God's kingdom. Jesus indentified anxiety as one of the greatest impediments to fulfilling our God-given destiny. One of the Enemy's great strategies to derail you from seeking God's kingdom is to fill you with anxiety.

Worry can cause us to miss out on experiencing not only God's purposes but his power. In Luke 8:4–15 Jesus described the Word of God as seeds scattered onto the soil of human hearts. These seeds are meant to sink deep, take root, and explode into a harvest of fruit. For some people, though, tender shoots grow just a bit before weeds choke them out, and the plant never reaches its potential. What is the weed that chokes out God's blessing in our lives? Jesus called it "life's worries" (v. 14 NIV). Many of us are missing out on the power of the Word of Life because it is being choked out by the worries of this life. If we desire to see a harvest of joy, peace, and blessing spring up in our hearts, we must find a way to uproot the weeds of worry.

A perpetually anxious state of mind can also propel us toward unhealthy ways of living. Anxiety about grades can lead you to dishonesty. Anxiety about dating can push you to make unhealthy compromises. Anxiety about finances can lead you to be unethical. Anxiety about being liked can lead you to embellish stories and act like someone you're not. Anxiety can propel you to seek comfort and refuge in a million different addictive, unhealthy behaviors.

Anxiety can even damage our physical health, like I experienced with my heart issues. Worries about hypothetical scenarios, about what may happen in the future, are actually killing us in the present.

If anxiety could be conquered, a mortal blow would be struck to many destructive habits in our lives.

Something else anxiety can cause—and this is the greatest tragedy of all—is missing out on simply enjoying God's presence. We see this message from Jesus in another moment when he connected the issues of anxiety and intimacy with God: when Mary sat and enjoyed a conversation with him while Martha frantically tended to the myriad household tasks.

In frustration Martha tried to get Mary to break away from time with Jesus in order to dive into domestic busyness. Jesus tenderly warned, "Martha, Martha, you are anxious and troubled about many things, but one thing is necessary. Mary has chosen the good portion, which will not be taken away from her" (Luke 10:41–42). Martha's worry-filled distraction led her to miss a unique moment of devotion.

Over and over the Scriptures contrast distracted anxiety and intentional intimacy. To indulge one is to forsake the other. This is why Jesus commanded people to pursue devotion and leave behind distraction. The Christian life is meant to be characterized by a lack of anxiety. And let me say, the world needs to see this from followers of Christ.

RELINQUISH ANXIETY AND PURSUE INTIMACY WITH GOD

The world is not impressed when we talk about the Prince of Peace and then live lives full of stress. In fact, one of the most attractive features of the believing community in the first century was their peaceful disposition, even in the face of persecution.

In the book *Cities and Bishoprics of Phrygia*, William Mitchell Ramsay described an inscription found in the ancient city of Phrygia that translates to *Titedios Amerimnos*. Ramsay suggested that Amerimnos may be a baptismal name given to a man named Titedios when he became a Christian, which was common practice for early believers. The name *Amerimnos* means someone who "takes no thought for the morrow,"[1] who possesses an undistracted mind. Perhaps when Titedios started his new life in Christ, he no longer panicked about the future or got stressed out about his task list. Maybe he became singularly focused on the one necessary thing, like Mary did, and sought first the kingdom of God, as Jesus described. He wasn't living distracted like he had been before.

This way of living is possible today. It's an offer on the table for us. Jesus does not simply want to command us not to be anxious. He wants to enable us to disentangle ourselves from the grip of anxiety. Jesus liberates us not only from sin and condemnation but also from worry.

So how do we experience this? In recent years many young believers have asked me how I manage stress and how I cultivate devotion to God. I give the same answer to both of those questions. I tell them that I live in Philippians chapter 4, where Paul actually said, "Do not be anxious about anything" (v. 6). Isn't that powerful?

Think about that for a moment: anxiety is never godly! There will never be a circumstance in which you are obligated to worry. Can that be a breath of fresh air to you? It does not mean you do not care about people or issues in your life. It means you don't need to be a slave to the stomach-knotting, scalp-drying, shoulder-tensing stress that some of us live with (and may even believe is virtuous). The Bible says no to that! There is no value in it at all. "Do not be anxious about anything."

The root of the word translated as "anxiety" in this verse means "to draw in different directions, distract." I don't know about you, but this is where my mind often goes as I lie in bed at night and when I wake up in the morning. Focus is an ever more rare commodity in our world today. Our minds naturally pinball among multiple issues with the inability to lock on to any one issue for a significant period of time. How do we break this pattern?

Well, Paul followed up "do not be anxious about anything" with "but in everything by prayer and supplication with thanksgiving let your requests be made known to God" (Philippians 4:6). Note the parallel: be anxious for *no* thing, but in *every* thing, let your requests be made known. Anxiety should be applied to no thing. But prayer should be applied to everything.

Now, I get that you might be rolling your eyes here. *That's the secret to solving anxiety, Ben? "Just pray more." Thanks. Super helpful.*

Before you criticize the theory, I invite you to compare it to your current method of coping. How are you managing stress in your life right now? For many of us, our verse might say, "Be anxious for nothing, but in everything eat a ton of sugar and carbs." Now, I'm not judging you. I get it. When we were first planting Passion City Church, DC, someone asked my wife and me what we were eating. Donna replied without hesitation, "Our feelings." Many of us are taking our cares to the pantry rather than to prayer!

Others of you may flee unpleasant feelings of stress by diving into social media and scrolling mindlessly. The sad irony is that social media is typically a source of more anxiety, not less. Or there may be myriad other addictions we turn to for escape. So before you prematurely dismiss the invitation from Scripture, you must honestly ask the question, *How is my current coping mechanism working for me?*

Interestingly there have been multiple articles in medical journals the past several years championing the health benefits of meditation and gratitude. I would say that modern science is stumbling upon an ancient path that has been available all along in Jesus.

Scripture can guide us toward our twin goals of relinquishing anxiety and pursuing intimacy with God. Paul gave us three steps in the process.*

1. RELEASE OUR WORRIES

First, *we release our worries to the Lord.* I love that Paul used the passive voice: "let your requests be made known." It makes it sound like they want to get out. We just need to let them!

If we are honest, many of us wake up with all manner of resentments, concerns, and uncertainties rolling around in our minds. As we get up and get ready for the day, these thoughts keep poking up to the surface of our conscious mind and we stuff them back deep down inside. We don't have time to think about them. So we eat our feelings, only to see them come up later as road rage or irritation with a coworker or impatience with our children. We are like a guy shoving a beach ball underwater—you can hold it down for a while, but it wants to come up, and when you slip, it flies up and hits you in the face.

God's first invitation here is simple: don't stuff those worries down. Let them surface. How do you do that? He tells us to do it "by prayer." Paul used a general term for creating space in your schedule to interact with God.

Now, I know some may object, "I don't have time for that." But I am going to challenge you to rethink that. There is a saying in sharpshooter

---

* Before we continue I'd like to clarify that, while the advice and biblical wisdom throughout this chapter can be helpful for everyone, some of us experience anxiety and other complex mental health issues that require clinical help. If you are sensing this could be the case for you, please don't hesitate to seek the guidance of a physician or professional counselor.

circles in the military: "Slow is smooth and smooth is fast." If you are firing a weapon and you rush the shot, you are likely going to miss the target. That means you must adjust and fire again, which in the end costs you more time. Haste costs you accuracy. For many of us this is true of our lives. Anxiety has made us busier but not more effective. If you give yourself the time to offload anxiety and think with clarity, you may just discover that you solve problems with greater efficiency.

For me this moment of releasing worries to the Lord fits best first thing in the morning before my children get up. If they wake me up, the combination of their youthful craziness and my simmering anxiety usually results in an elevated heart rate and a high potential for me to say things I have to apologize for later. So I rise early and quickly get to a quiet room. Then I follow Paul's prescribed pattern and begin with supplication.

The word *supplication* means to present a need. I tend to get specific. I have found it most helpful for me to write these prayers in a journal. Something about moving my hand on a piece of paper and listing out my concerns feels like I am truly getting them out of me and on a page in front of me and to the Lord. I externalize my problems.

While doing this I give unfettered license to my inner voice. I do not attempt to control the flow of my thoughts or try to clean up the words and make them sound prettier or more acceptable. I just vomit up whatever is inside. If I'm all over the place with my concerns and feelings, that's okay. If my words would sound weird or embarrassing to anyone else who might listen, fine. I do not try to regulate what comes up from within in these quiet moments with God.

If this sounds silly to you at all, don't forget: all intimacy requires honesty. If you are not real with another person, you cannot have a real relationship. And the same is true with God. Look through the Scriptures at those who enjoyed a deep fellowship with God. Often their moments of greatest intimacy began in a moment of brutal or uncomfortable honesty. Sometimes where we are is not where we want to be. But you have to start where you are.

David got real with God in the cave and watched his worry become worship (Psalm 57, 142).

Abraham vented his pain to God in prayer and walked away gripping God's promise (Genesis 15).

Elijah lamented his loneliness and God fed him, cared for him, and showed him his protégé (1 Kings 19).

Jesus poured out his soul in the garden of Gethsemane and found the strength to say, "Not my will, but yours, be done" (Luke 22:42).

In certain seasons I have found it helpful to write at the top of the page, *How do you feel?* Then I put words around those feelings. Often this begins a process of helping me uncover what concerns lie underneath the surface. I will write, *I feel anxious.* Then I do what King David taught us to do. I question the emotional state of my soul: *"Why are you cast down, O my soul?"* (Psalm 42:5).

I remember writing one morning, *I am stressed.*

Why? I asked myself.

Because of the sermon I have to preach tonight.

A new thought occurred to me: *What are you afraid of? Are you afraid that God's purposes will be thwarted? Are you terrified that he won't be glorified?*

I realized, *No, it's not that.*

Then an unguarded thought rose up: *I'm afraid I won't be glorified. I want them to think I'm smart, funny, wise, and gifted so I will feel better about myself.*

Whoa. Validation is not the purpose of a sermon! With a sermon I am meant to feed the sheep and benefit them, not use the sheep to feed my ego and benefit myself.

Creating this space to get honest allowed me to see the root of my anxiety and apply the truth in the deep place. I needed to believe again that I was loved and accepted by God, so when I stepped onstage it was with the confidence that came from the pure motive to bless, not the inferior motive to impress.

If we look again at Philippians 4:6, we'll see that Paul said to pray about worries "with thanksgiving." Why would we be thankful in the midst of telling God all our fears and concerns? One simple reason: because we are invited to let our requests be made known *to God*! You and I have the opportunity to pour out our concerns to the one Being who can do something supernatural and decisive about it!

I love these two passages because they issue the same command, but give us two different motivations:

> "Cast all your anxiety on him because he cares for you" (1 Peter 5:7 niv).
>
> "Cast your burden on the LORD, and he will sustain you; he will never permit the righteous to be moved" (Psalm 55:22).

Both of these verses call us to cast our cares upon the Lord. One says to do it because he is strong enough to carry them. The other tells us to do it because he is loving enough to want to.

Once when my oldest daughter, Hannah, was about five years old, I picked her up to carry her up the stairs. She immediately protested, "No, Daddy! I'm too heavy." This caught me off guard for a moment. *Who had told her she was too heavy?* So I hoisted her up with one arm, looked her in the eye, and whispered, "You are not too heavy for Daddy, baby."

I don't know what burdens you are carrying today, but they are not too heavy for your Father. And neither are you. You may be tasked with carrying a heavy burden in this season of your life, but your God wants to carry *you*. Let that knowledge have a profound effect on your well-being.

Paul described the implications of this outpouring of our concerns in the following verse: "The peace of God, which surpasses all understanding, will guard your hearts and your minds in Christ Jesus" (Philippians 4:7). When you place your cares into the hands of the King, an otherworldly calm that extends beyond human comprehension will step in front of your heart's door like a bouncer. It will refuse to let anxieties past the velvet rope into the exclusive inner sanctum of your heart and mind.

One remarkable example of this happened during the Civil War. As General Robert E. Lee led his army of 76,000 men into Pennsylvania, panic took hold of Washington, DC. Amid the chaos, President Abraham Lincoln remained strangely confident. He later related to a general wounded at Gettysburg: "When everyone seemed panic-stricken . . . I went to my room . . . and got down on my knees before Almighty God and prayed . . . Soon a sweet comfort crept into my soul that God Almighty had taken the whole business into His own hands."[2]

In the midst of impossible stress, the president was free to function because the supernatural peace available in Christ Jesus set a garrison around his heart. Prayer does not release you from having to make decisions, but it does free you up to make good decisions.

A few years ago my sister, who is a counselor, and a friend, who is a Navy SEAL, both recommended I try monitoring my heart rate variability. Hearing the exact same recommendation from both a counselor and a SEAL, I figured I should check it out.

In layman's terms, a heart rate variability monitor does not simply track your heart rate (beats per minute), but measures the time between beats as well. This measurement of your heart's rhythm indicates how emotional states are affecting your nervous system and your ability to concentrate. A display on my phone shows my *coherence*, or how calm my mental state is as reflected in the consistency of my heart rate. Over the course of several months, I was amazed to see how accurate this device was. When I felt stressed and scatterbrained, my coherence monitor reflected it immediately. The little dial would turn bright red (not good) and the little graph would look erratic. When I was calm, the lines would even out and the monitor would turn a pleasant shade of green.

Over time I found that I consistently registered in the red zone when I first put the monitor on. But if I inhaled and exhaled slowly and wrote down whatever stressful thought came to mind, then slowly led my mind back to something pleasant, my coherence score would jump up. And I would feel calmer, less anxious, and more able to focus on the work ahead of me.

I found that dedicating even a few minutes to pausing, breathing, and casting my anxieties upon the Lord actually allowed me to be more productive with the next several hours of the day. Rather than my mind skipping wildly from studies to texts to emails to random scrolling online, I could center on a single task and accomplish it.

Take, for example, my devotional reading. If I sat down and tried to read the Scriptures right away, I found concentration and retention to be entirely elusive. But if I spent five minutes stilling my mind, writing down my anxieties, and breathing slowly and calmly, then I could focus and engage with the Word of God.

Jeremiah Burroughs, in his Puritan classic *The Rare Jewel of Christian Contentment*, used two wonderful illustrations to make this point.

First, he explained how you cannot pour wine into a shaky bottle.

You must first hold the bottle still and then you can pour in the wine. The same is true with blessings from God. Be still if you would have mercy poured into your soul.

Second, he said that when a child wants something, you will not give it to them when they are losing their minds. You'll make them first be still, even if you intend to give them the thing all along. You want them to compose themselves first. God is a good parent like this. Be still and wait. It honors him to do this.[3]

Once we have cast out our worries, we find that we are ready to receive God's Word. Emptying our minds of anxiety is not sufficient— that is just the first step to gaining clarity and strength of mind. This is where many modern meditation practices fall short. True spirituality is not simply the absence of the negative, but the presence of the positive! We cast off one set of thoughts so we can pick up another. This is the second step. We release our worries so that we can embrace God's Word. We lay down our troubles so that our minds can lay hold of God's truth.

2. EMBRACE GOD'S WORD

Scripture leaves no question about where we need to turn our focus. Paul said, "Don't worry about anything. . . . Fix your thoughts on what is true, and honorable, and right, and pure, and lovely, and admirable. *Think about* things that are excellent and worthy of praise" (Philippians 4:6, 8 NLT).

We saw the same message in Jesus' words earlier in this chapter: "Do not worry, saying, 'What shall we eat?' . . . But seek first his kingdom and his righteousness" (Matthew 6:31–33 NIV).

This is the rhythm advocated in the Scriptures. We are meant to release our worries to him; then we are able to embrace his truth with our minds. We replace our anxious thoughts with beautiful, motivational thoughts about him.

WE LAY DOWN OUR TROUBLES SO WE CAN LAY HOLD OF GOD'S TRUTH.

Throughout my twenties I developed the habit of writing in my journal with two colored pens. At first I would write out my unfiltered thoughts in blue. Then, when all my anxious thoughts were spent, I took up a black pen. I wanted a color that was deeper and more substantial. With my black pen I would write out verses of Scripture. Writing out the words forced me to move slowly through a passage. Over the course of months, I wrote out multiple books of the Bible, but in the normal flow of a morning I would write out maybe two or three verses at a time.

Then I would take my blue pen and write my response to God's Word. I wanted my thoughts and emotions to bend around and rest upon the enduring Word of God. I wanted his thinking to shape my own.

This rhythm helped me accomplish the dual calling of Jesus—to cast off distractions, and then, with a calm mind, pursue an undistracted devotion to him. I still look back fondly on those days. My knowledge of God expanded. My trust of God deepened. And my love of God exploded. I want this for you.

Over time I have developed other ways of cultivating this kind of intimacy with him as well. I categorize my habits under two headings: consistency and creativity. I have a consistent time I meet with the Lord each morning, but I also try to sprinkle into my schedule creative ways to cultivate intimacy with the Lord. I take prayer walks on the weekend. Once a month I take a full "Day with the Lord," when I go to a unique location and spend the day reading and praying. I've spent days with the Lord at the beach, in the woods, at a monastery, in an empty football stadium, or, when I was younger, on the roof of a local high school!

Take a minute now and ask the Lord what meeting with him consistently and creatively might look like for you. Maybe you'll listen to an audio Bible on the way to work, then use the drive home to pray. Perhaps you'll read a devotional book before you go to bed. Maybe you'll do what a friend of mine does and periodically take walks in a graveyard, contemplating the brevity of life (personally, I've always had a hard time with that one). Maybe you'll map out a spiritual retreat once a month or quarter.

Keep in mind that if you love someone, you'll find ways to spend time with them. So pray and ask the Lord what it might look like for you to steal away with him periodically. Where could you go? What could you do?

3. LIVE OUT WHAT YOU'VE LEARNED

Whatever and wherever you do this, the insights you glean are not meant to stay locked up in that quiet place. These moments with God are meant to work their way through your mind, into your heart, and then out through your life.

This last part is where Paul ended his exhortation in Philippians 4. After releasing worry and embracing God's Word, we are meant to walk out what we have learned. He wrote, "What you have learned and received and heard and seen in me—practice these things, and the God of peace will be with you" (v. 9).

When we release our anxiety, the peace of God will guard us. And when we walk in his ways, the God of peace will be with us. He does not simply send his peace into our hearts. He walks alongside us in our lives and empowers us to live a supernatural life.

In 1993 a small, elite force of US troops were sent into Mogadishu, Somalia, to capture two high-value targets. In the course of the operation, two Black Hawk helicopters were shot down. Suddenly an operation that was meant to last less than an hour turned into an overnight firefight with US troops surrounded by thousands of Somali soldiers. The events of that day are recorded in the book *Black Hawk Down*, which later became a movie.[4]

Twenty-four-year-old Army Ranger Sergeant Jeff Struecker led the three-vehicle convoy that returned multiple times into the firefight to rescue wounded or stranded soldiers. The first US casualty in the operation occurred in his Humvee. Struecker's friend Sergeant Pilla was killed. Miraculously, Struecker led the column of Humvees out of the city and into the safety of the military base.

Upon arrival, he was informed that there were still men trapped in the city and that he would have to drive back into the chaos. A member of Delta approached him and told him he would have to wash the blood out of the back of his vehicle before he returned to pick up the men. Forcing them to sit in the blood of their friend would be too traumatic.

Struecker recounted in a speech years later that he experienced a moment of panic as he washed his friend's blood from the rear of the vehicle. He said a thought kept racing through his mind: *This will be my blood. This will be my blood.* He did not have it in him to return, but he knew he had to.

He paused for a moment to pray. While he was praying, a new thought entered his mind: *God determines whether I live or die—God and not anyone else. If he chooses to allow me to survive today, I will go home to my wife. If I die, then I go to my heavenly home with Jesus. Either way, I am going home.*

As he took that moment to cast his anxieties upon the Lord, then reflect upon the sovereignty of God and his salvation through Jesus, he experienced a calm settle in his spirit.

He jumped back in the driver's seat, returned to the city, and evacuated more men. Then he did it again. And again. And in the following days, he was able to comfort the grieving soldiers with the same comfort that he had received in his hour of need. A supernatural peace enabled him to live a heroically selfless life.[5]

Though I pray you will never experience anything like what these soldiers endured, I want you to know that this same spiritual practice that worked for Sergeant Struecker can work for you. When we release our worry and take up God's Word, we can engage the work he lays before us with a peace that surpasses description.

• • •

Before we finish this chapter, let me close with a story from one of my favorite autobiographies, *John G. Paton: Missionary to the New Hebrides*.

Paton served as a missionary to a chain of islands in the South Pacific called the New Hebrides, now known as Vanuatu. The book reads like an action movie. Paton routinely dodged hatchets aimed at his head and evaded gunfire. On more than one occasion, he grabbed hold of a native who was attempting to kill him and hugged the man tightly until he agreed to stop trying to murder him!

At one point a group of men surrounded Paton's hut and called him out to be killed. Realizing he could not escape, Paton prayed for a moment, then marched out to the men and rebuked them for being inhospitable! That completely took them off guard. Stunned for a moment, they felt convicted and agreed. They confessed that it was rude of them to attempt to kill him, and from then on they would only kill others on his behalf. That was not really Paton's goal, but it was a start.

Before his time in the New Hebrides concluded, Paton saw the entire island of Aniwa come to Christ. Today, over one hundred years after his death, 85 percent of the population still identifies as Christian.[6]

At one point when he discovered a plot to kill him, he was instructed by a chief to hide in a tree. He wrote:

> Being entirely at the mercy of such doubtful and vacillating friends, I, though perplexed, felt it best to obey. I climbed into the tree and was left there alone in the bush. The hours I spent there live all before me as if it were but of yesterday.
>
> I heard the frequent discharging of muskets, and the yells of the [people below]. Yet I sat there among the branches, as safe as in the arms of Jesus. Never, in all my sorrows, did my Lord draw nearer to me, and speak more soothingly in my soul, than when the moonlight flickered among those chestnut leaves, and the night air played on my throbbing brow, as I told all my heart to Jesus. Alone, yet not alone! If it be to glorify my God, I will not grudge to spend many nights alone in such a tree, to feel again my Savior's spiritual presence, to enjoy His consoling fellowship. If thus thrown back upon your own soul, alone, all alone, in the midnight, in the bush, in the very embrace of death itself, have you a Friend that will not fail you then?[7]

This amazing peace is available to all of us who are, in Paul's words, "in Christ Jesus" (Philippians 4:7). Will you take up the offer to rest in the peace of God that surpasses all understanding?

RHYTHMS OF REST

1. Take a moment and write down a few places where you could go to spend time alone with God.
2. Then, write down a time of day that would work for you to do this.

3. Now, think about a plan for how you might spend that time. Consider writing out Philippians 4 (or the whole book of Philippians!). Or, head to restandwar.com for some devotional ideas.

4. Do you have some anxieties you can cast upon God now?

CHAPTER 10

PRODUCTIVE SCHEDULE

Several years ago I visited the Navy SEAL base on Coronado Island, off the coast of San Diego. While I was there one of the guys invited me to take on the SEAL obstacle course. It was a *challenge.*

I spent the next several grueling minutes leaping over walls, climbing nets and ropes, balancing, swinging, and sweating until I finally crossed the finish line. To my astonishment, I completed it in twelve minutes, just under the maximum time allowed to qualify to be a SEAL. I felt amazing.

Then my friend from the SEAL team ran the course. He completed it in six minutes, while walking leisurely between each obstacle. I told myself, *Well, he's had more practice.* Then I immediately thought, *And, let's be honest, he's a Navy SEAL!* When I needed to take nine ibuprofen a day for the next two weeks simply to function, I realized that God did not build me to be a SEAL. I am finely tuned to read books.

I am honored and challenged whenever I visit the SEAL community, but I always walk away rolling through a mental checklist of things I need to do to be more of a man. Now, none of the SEALs have ever put that pressure on me. They have never written me a prescription to up my manliness quotient. But it is impossible to leave that environment and not think about manliness and how much of it you have.

Usually it begins with me asking myself questions like, *Why am I not proficient with an M4 yet?* Or, *What would my first move be in a knife fight? I don't even know!* Or, *What if I am in a situation where I need to fly a helicopter? I'm going to be stuck looking for a real man to come save the day! What's wrong with me?*

My mind will be on this track for days, until I realize that Navy SEALs cannot be the standard for manliness. That would mean there are not a lot of men in the world.

Then that raises a question: What does a man do? How do I know if I'm doing it? I know what a phone does. I know what a hammer does. What does a man do? What is the standard someone has to meet in order for us to say, "That is what a man is meant to do"?

Our modern answers are insufficient. We say things like, "Just do what you love," or, "Do what you are good at." But this is incomplete. No criterion for the meaning of life is sufficient if a serial killer could fulfill it: "I'm good at killing people, and frankly, I enjoy it." *Yikes.* No, we need a higher calling than this. We need a more inspired, more objective, and morally robust answer to the purpose of a person.

I believe if we can answer this question, a cloud of despair could lift off an entire generation. Viktor Frankl, the Auschwitz survivor and author of *Man's Search for Meaning*, said, "People today have the means to live, but no meaning to live for."[1] I talk to so many people who struggle with a sense of meaninglessness in their day-to-day lives. Get up, get dressed, go to work, buy things, watch a screen, sleep, repeat. Meaninglessness stalks the modern man and woman. We need a compelling *why* to inform and shape all the various *whats* we engage in throughout the day. Philosopher Friedrich Nietzsche said, "He who has a Why to live for can bear almost any How."[2] We need to know our why.

Let's start with this thought: to understand a creation, we would do well to look to its creator's intent. Our *why* for the day-to-day goes back to why we are here at all. Our "meaning to live for" is tied to fulfilling the purpose we were made for.

OUR PURPOSE FROM THE BEGINNING

So what does God intend for a man to do? To answer that question, we need to go back to the beginning. Genesis 1 tells us that we are made in the image of God. Now, scholars debate what that means exactly, and we will not discuss that exhaustively here. But I do want to show you something that is true of God that we are meant to mirror, or image, as we engage the world.

Genesis 1:2 says, "The earth was [formless] and void, and darkness was over the face of the deep." Scholars agree that these four descriptors—*formless, void, darkness*, and *the deep*—are perceived as negative. Scripture doesn't tell us where this negative situation came from. The author's goal is not to tell us everything about creation; it is to show us the God of creation. Moses wanted us to understand what God cares about and what he is like.

So while much can and should be said about what's happening here, let me focus your attention on two words: *formless* and *void*. They are the Hebrew words *tohu* and *bohu*, which kind of sound like a clown duo. The first word means "without structure or order." The second means "without content." There is nothing filling it. You could think of *tohu* as, "There is no vase," and *bohu* as, "There are no flowers in the vase."

Biblical scholar David Tsumura described this as "an unproductive and uninhabited place."[3] The world was a structureless, watery matrix that was not conducive to life. No structure and no life. No form and no flourishing.

Then, the Spirit of God began to hover over the surface of this primordial abyss. God exerted himself on the dark waters of chaos. In a stunning display of power, he spoke light into existence and began to rotate this watery matrix (a day is one rotation of the earth on its axis). On day two, as the waters spun, they separated into sea and air. The waters continued to recede, and by day three, dry land appeared.

In three days God created sea, air, and land. He formed the teleological structures needed to support life. He solved the problem of *tohu*!

After examining the quality of these static life-support systems and calling them "good," God turned his attention to solving the second problem: *bohu*.

Look closely and you'll see beautiful symmetry in his work. In the first three days he created the various structures conducive for life, then in the final three days of creation he filled each structure:

Day 1: light

Day 2: sky and the seas

Day 3: land

Day 4: the bearers of the light (sun, stars)

Day 5: the birds that fill the air and fish to fill the sea

Day 6: land animals and human beings

God saw the problem of *tohu* and *bohu*, formlessness and a void, the lack of structure and lack of life, and he answered by bringing form and then fullness. He created order, but not a stiff, stifling order. He created organic, dynamic structures that contain what is necessary to promote the flourishing of all life! This is our God. He creates structure, then fills it with content. Form for the sake of fullness. Order so that life may flourish.

The narrative of Genesis 1 shifts as we near the end of it. We read that God declared to himself, "'Let us make man in our image, after our likeness'" (v. 26). And then, "God created man in his own image, in the image of God he created him; male and female he created them" (v. 27).

At the close of chapter 1 we find out what God was doing all this for. He did it for us.

STRUCTURE THAT LEADS
TO FLOURISHING

Years ago a pastor friend of mine got engaged to a beautiful young woman. During the months of their engagement, he built all the furniture for their home. By hand. I can't even put together a desk from IKEA, but he was out in the woods sizing up trees, thinking, *That looks like it'll make a good coffee table.* Then he'd set to work on it with an axe.

The man built bed frames, end tables, a coffee table, and numerous other pieces. On the evening before their wedding, I stood in his living room surrounded by them all and marveled at what he had done. From the creativity in his mind, by the strength of his arm, and because of the love in his heart, he'd built a home for himself and his bride. He'd prepared a place where they could share life together. Build memories. Laugh. Cry. Grow closer. It was beautiful. He'd built all this structure so they could celebrate life together.

This is exactly what God was up to in Genesis 1 and 2. With the creativity in his mind, by the strength of his power, and because of the love in his heart, God built a garden and he named it "delight." He placed humanity within it so they might live with him.

The first full day for the man and woman was the Sabbath day of rest. First things came first: celebrating God by rejoicing in what he made, and enjoying relationship with him and with each other. God built a home for humanity so they could make memories and enjoy the gift of life with him.

Next, in Genesis 2, we see something interesting: the story of creation is retold, but not chronologically. While Adam and Eve are presented as the sixth creative event in Genesis 1, they are the thematically central part of the story in Genesis 2. And as the story of creation is told from a more relationship-centered point of view, we learn more of what humanity is meant to be up to. The man and woman were made to enjoy God—but they also had a job to do! They were made not only for intimacy but also for impact! God did not intend to be the only one working.

Genesis 2, like chapter 1, begins with a negative situation: "When no bush of the field was yet in the land and no small plant of the field had yet sprung up—for the LORD God had not caused it to rain on the land, and there was no man to work the ground" (v. 5).

Notice the repetition of *no*: no bush, no plant, no rain, no man. The creation had not reached its potential because humanity had not arrived on the scene. So God created the man and placed him in the garden. Here, in this context, we discover humanity's calling: "The LORD God took the man and put him in the Garden of Eden to cultivate it and tend it" (v. 15 NASB).

What does it mean to cultivate a piece of land? It means you rearrange the raw materials present to create an environment where crops can flourish. Adam was called to exert himself on the unrefined earth before him and, by his power, organize it in a way that maximized its potential. Till the soil, water the crops, and feed the livestock so that all living things could be fruitful. To cultivate means to build structure so that life can flourish.

If you're thinking this sounds familiar, you are right. God built structures that are conducive to flourishing. Then he made male and female in his image. In this sense we are meant to be like him. We are meant to create an environment where life can flourish. An integral part of our creation mandate is exerting our energy on the raw materials he's given us in order to make them maximally fruitful under God.

We are cultivators. We bring order where there is none—not a stifling order, but a structure that supports the flourishing of life. This is our life's mission, an ongoing quest. This is a central part of why you and I are here.

This involves removing some things that are extraneous, inefficient, or unhelpful. It means adding some things that are beneficial. And it means organizing and arranging things so they can be maximally fruitful.

If I am cultivating a vineyard, I have to prune some branches to encourage it to grow properly. I also must add sunlight, water, mineral-rich soil. I have to study what elements encourage the growth of vines and introduce those elements into the environment.

Then I need structure. It's not only a matter of addition and subtraction, but organization too. I tie these vines to trellises—not in a torturous way, but in a way that keeps the vines out of the dirt so they can grow strong and develop fruit.

I use my wisdom, strength, and care to add, subtract, and organize in such a way that the vine—the life—I am committed to can flourish and reach its full potential. This is what it means to cultivate.

And this is what a man or woman does!

WE ARE MEANT TO CREATE AN ENVIRONMENT WHERE LIFE CAN FLOURISH.

WHAT YOU'RE MEANT TO DO

This is what Moses did. When he led the people of Israel out of the land of Egypt, they were a ragged mob of former slaves. As they journeyed through the wild places, he began to form this loose confederation of tribes into ranks. Though there was much drama along the way, by the time Joshua was ready to lead them across the Jordan River, they were organized enough to be victorious in their quest for the promised land.

This is what kings and leaders do. They build structure—cities, towns, a system of roads, methods of communication, legislative bodies, and clear, just laws. Proverbs tells us that when a wise king rules, the people rejoice (29:2). Why? Because these "forms" allow the people to flourish. They create structures that help us meet basic needs, raise children in safety, and utilize our God-given abilities without constant fear of threats or attack. Just think: you do not vacation in a lawless country. Forms bring freedom. Structure benefits life.

This is what Jesus did for us. When Satan tempted Adam and Eve, he invited chaos back onto the scene. When Jesus arrived, he announced that he had come to establish a kingdom. What is a kingdom? It is a system of rule under a king. He was saying, "I am bringing a new order—a new structure. I am bringing a system built on grace that liberates women and men to step into the fullness of who they were meant to be under God."

This is what people are doing all around us today. Architects and engineers create physical structures that will stand strong and allow us to live and work in them. Financial managers invest our money in a way that maximizes its potential. Teachers organize curricula and classrooms so that children can learn and grow.

Husbands organize their time, money, and energy in a way that creates an environment for their wives to flourish under God. Wives do the same for husbands. Parents deploy resources in a way that allows their children to prosper. Bosses create work environments that equip their employees to maximize their talents and passions in the pursuit of a common goal.

Structure for the sake of flourishing. Form for the sake of fullness. Order that is conducive to the flourishing of life. This is the calling of a man and a woman.

You are not meant to just "do you" or try to eke out a modicum of happiness before you disappear. You are meant to exert your God-given gifts on the God-given raw materials at your disposal for the good of others and the glory of God. The living creatures around you are to flourish because of your cultivation, *because you exist*.

You are meant to do this for yourself too—to exercise dominion over your schedule and allocate your resources so that your gifts, passions, and energies reach their full potential under God.

BE THE MASTER OF YOUR CALENDAR

How do we go about what we are on earth to do? We need a plan of attack. We need to harness our calendar for the greatest of all causes. We need to organize our days.

This may not sound particularly spiritual or profound. But what I am advocating is not simply putting dates on the calendar. I am calling us to order our world, and it begins with deciding what we'll put our hands to throughout the day. This is not simply about the modern practice of keeping a calendar. This is about figuring out how to sync up eternity in our heart with the wristwatch on our arm.

Lack of preparation opens us up to the dual attack of unproductivity and stress. We feel like we have so much to do but also do not know what to do. So we check our email or social media two hundred times a day, or take long lunches that have no strategic purpose. We feel busy but not productive. We are like an octopus on roller skates. There is plenty of movement, but it is not necessarily forward!

Several years ago I read a book that discussed lion tamers. The author set out to answer this question: Why do animal trainers carry a four-legged stool when they go into a cage of lions? We understand what the whip is for. We get the pistol—that's for if things end up not really working out. But why the stool?

The answer was fascinating: "He holds the stool by the back and thrusts the legs toward the face of the wild animal. Those who know maintain that the animal tries to focus on all four legs at once. In the attempt to focus on all four, a kind of paralysis overwhelms the animal, and it becomes tame, weak, and disabled because its attention is fragmented."[4]

Some of us look just like this. We're doing a bunch of random activity, or we've got analysis paralysis. But we are meant to live far more purposeful and productive lives!

I have heard people say that Jesus had a ministry of interruptions. I absolutely disagree. Jesus did not go around letting other people set the agenda of his day. He often told people no—more than you might guess.

The morning after a late night of healing people, the disciples pressured Jesus to get back into town and keep healing. The people were demanding it. But Jesus' answer was no. He told them he must preach, so they would be moving on. The crowds did not hand him his cause; his Father did. And miracles were meant to authenticate the message.

He preached and healed in Capernaum. Then it was time to head to the next spot.

A man tried to slow him down once, basically saying, "I want to follow you, but let me bury my dad first." Jesus said, "Let the dead bury their own dead" (Matthew 8:19–22 NIV), and he kept walking. He didn't even break stride!

When another cried out, "Tell my brother to divide the inheritance with me," Jesus responded, "Who appointed me . . . an arbiter between you?" (Luke 12:13–14 NIV). This guy was trying to set Jesus' agenda, and Jesus wasn't having it. *Arbiter* was not on his list of identities.

However, when a blind man cried out, "Son of David, have mercy on me," Jesus stopped in his tracks and called the man to him (Matthew 20). Why? Because that request aligned with Jesus' strategic purpose. He was the Son of David and he had come to give mercy. The activity matched his identity.

Jesus was willing to adapt his schedule but not outside the boundaries of his calling.

Jesus was not wandering around spouting quotable lines and randomly hanging with people. He was methodically, strategically implementing a plan for the global spread of his message. And he executed his plan brilliantly. He set his agenda by priority, not proximity, and we are meant to do the same.

You and I have been commissioned by God Almighty himself to steward his creation. We need to learn how to be strategic like Jesus was, to set our agenda by priority, to get serious about stewarding what God has given us the very best we can.

Paul told the Ephesians to "[make] the most of every opportunity, because the days are evil" (Ephesians 5:16 NIV). Life is too precious to waste time. We are meant to leverage every moment for redemptive purpose.

Proverbs 12:24 states, "The hand of the diligent will rule." We are meant to be rulers in our environments, not victims. And diligence is an essential, celebrated, and commanded quality of rulers.

Jesus told the parable of the managers entrusted with talents (Matthew 25). The master expected his managers to take those talents and invest them in a way that would be maximally profitable. This was an illustration of our lives under God. We have been given days. We have been given resources. We have been given talents. And we are meant to organize them in such a way that yields the maximum potential out of all life under our care.

This stewardship begins with our own lives, by cultivating ourselves.

So say this with me: "I am not the victim of my schedule. I am the master."

Say it out loud. "I am not the victim of my schedule. I am the master."

Say it like you believe it!

This is neither arrogance nor wishful thinking. This is the child of God raising his or her voice to agree with the Maker's command.

Take the resources within your reach and maximize their potential.

Start by harnessing your time.

WHO WE ARE DETERMINES WHAT WE DO

Planning helps keep our priorities present in our practices. It reduces stress and it helps us get more done and miss out on fewer opportunities.

So to begin, we start with our titles. We begin with who we are. Our activity is meant to flow from our identity. Boxers box. Dancers dance. Students study (theoretically). Whatever identity you believe is most fundamental to who you are will determine how you conduct yourself in this world.

I encourage you to follow an exercise I did with interns when I served as a youth pastor. I gave them titles that were tied to the directives of our ministry—evangelist, counselor, teacher, servant, and worshiper. These five identities became the headings under which every activity of their week was organized. We gave them a piece of paper with these titles listed as headings at the top of the page, and underneath each heading they listed all the tasks they could think of. More than just a long to-do list, it helped them see how the work they were doing tied directly to their reason for being there.

Then we gave them a second sheet of paper with the seven days of the week broken down into thirty-minute increments. At the beginning of each week, they took their tasks listed under their titles and put them into a specific time of the week.

What first appeared to them to be a tedious act of calendaring ended up becoming their favorite part of the week! Something about seeing their eternal purposes touch down on specific times of their week filled their souls with something we struggle to define but desperately need: a sense of purpose.

I promise you that when you see the eternal touch the mundane, it will thrill your soul with a sense of meaning. I want that for you. And it starts here. Identifying your titles. Listing your tasks. Organizing your time.

I personally do this same practice I taught those interns. In the current season of my life, I am in the role of pastor of a church, so my titles look like this: Teacher. Leader. Administrator. Pastor/Shepherd. Then I include a fifth column for Child of God, and under it I place the subheadings Husband, Father, and Steward of our Financial Resources. During my devotional time on Monday mornings or Sunday nights, I fill out these two sheets.

By strategically planning out my weeks, I've discovered I am able to be fully present in every moment. I don't listen to a friend tell a story while my mind is on the phone calls I need to make. I know I'll return calls later, from 3:00 to 4:00 p.m., so in the present moment with my friend, I can be all his. I like having an undivided mind. Jim Elliot said it best: "Wherever you are, be all there."[5] Scheduling helps me live into this. By giving each task its space, I allow my mind to be fully engaged in whatever moment I am in. This simple rhythm of deciding when tasks will occur in advance brings an enormous sense of relief. There is freedom in this kind of order. There is peace in structure.

This is where being students and stewards of ourselves becomes so crucial. I've realized that I am a more patient and loving dad if I can get up and sit quietly with the Lord before my kids wake up. So that's what I do every morning.

A CLOSER LOOK AT MY SCHEDULE

I will go ahead and share with you the schedule I've found works for me, and along the way I'll point out how being a student of myself helped me become a better steward of myself.

Usually my time with the Lord in the morning flows naturally into strategic planning for the day and for the ministry I lead. At 7:30 a.m. I grab breakfast with the kids. We read a passage of Scripture and discuss, then they are out the door by 7:50 a.m. and I am back in the study at 8:00 a.m. I have discovered that my mind is most creative in the mornings, so every weekday I dedicate 8:00 to 11:00 a.m. to sermon writing and strategic thinking.

Frequent interruptions from texts or emails destroy the flow of creative thinking in those hours. So I instructed my staff, "Do not reach out to me at all from eight to eleven every weekday morning.

If you have a question, write it down. It can wait." I've also stopped checking emails in the morning. I always found that it put me into a reactive mindset rather than a creative one, and it was not a good use of my time.

But as a leader, I need to give my staff vision and offer myself to them as a resource so they can accomplish their goals for our organization. So I place meetings with leaders at 1:00 p.m. on Mondays and Wednesdays. On Monday we have a meeting that sets and clarifies the agenda and allows them to get the direction they need from me to execute their plans with confidence that week. Wednesday is a brief check-in to answer any clarifying questions. I lead best coming out of my thinking times in the mornings, so I stack those meetings in the 1:00 to 3:00 p.m. zone. I rarely do lunch meetings now. I realized they typically ate up two hours, even though the meeting was usually about solving a problem that only required fifteen minutes.

My counseling meetings are scheduled in the 2:00 to 4:00 p.m. range on weekdays. Usually by three o'clock I can't think creatively or strategically anymore, but I can listen. These are great times for me to pastor our people. I also stand out in front of our church on Sundays after each gathering and answer questions anyone may have.

Sometimes people ask if we can grab lunch to talk. I have gotten in the habit of telling them no—not to be rude, but because I just know it probably won't happen. I tell them, "I can't promise an hour or two down the road. But I am all yours right now. How can I help you?" Normally, all they want from me can be given to them right there. Only occasionally will someone have a problem that is so acute and specific to my skill set that we'll need to meet during the week.

From 4:00 to 5:00 p.m. I work out.

I allow myself one night out a week with church activities. Every other night I am with my kids. From 5:00 to 8:00 p.m. on those nights, I am 100 percent dad. I turn off the phone and put it away. In this current season my kids go to bed between 7:00 and 8:00 p.m., so that means I only get two to three hours with them on weekdays. I am not going to lose that time to a phone call or email or a TV show. The screens go off. We do homework and eat dinner and share our best, worst, and weirdest moments of the day. Then we read a book together and pray before bed.

From 8:00 to 9:00 p.m. I catch up with Donna about our day. We usually sit out on the back porch and talk. Then from 9:00 to 10:00 p.m. I get ready for bed. I don't take screens into our bedroom since they disrupt sleep patterns. Instead, I write a few sentences in a journal, spend a few moments reflecting on the day in prayer, and read two to three pages of a biography. And by 10:00 p.m., Lord willing, I am out.

Fridays are my days off. I use them to handle a lot of the family stewardship stuff we need to get done.

Saturdays are my day of rest. I stay off the iPad and computer— they remind me too much of work! I read a book I like. We go on adventures as a family. Sometimes an adventure is heading out to find a waterfall at a state park, or it's a walk around the neighborhood. But the kids know that Saturday I am theirs.

It is common for us to have twelve meals a week together as a family: six breakfasts and six dinners. My kids are young and I know it will not always be this way, so I don't want to miss these moments.

Does this automation of my schedule stifle creativity? No. It liberates me to channel my creative thinking toward the projects and plans I care about. I don't have to spend decision-making power each day figuring out when to get up or when to schedule meetings. It is already done. When we organize our time and resources in a way that is efficient and productive, we are free to invest our energy where it really matters: building up our family and friends. That's why we do it. We calendar as a way of loving the people around us. We structure so that they can flourish.

Take a moment before you move on to the next chapter and let the reality sink in that you have a divine calling under God. Your life has extraordinary purpose. You are meant to image God by organizing the resources he has given you so that all the life under your care, including your own, can flourish.

Then ask yourself, How can I cultivate my life this week? What needs to go into my schedule? What needs to come out? What needs to be restructured so I can be maximally fruitful in the hours God has given me?

Try making a list of your titles and organizing your tasks beneath them. Then see how they might fit into the time God has given you. I pray that you will experience the joy and deep satisfaction of seeing meaning fill the mundane and eternity touch earth.

RHYTHMS OF REST

1. How can you rearrange your schedule to cultivate and maximize your potential? What needs to be removed from your schedule? What needs to be added? What needs to be rearranged?
2. Try the exercise described in the previous section: make a list of your titles, then write out all your tasks beneath them.
3. Take a weekly calendar and see if you can schedule your activities by priority and not simply proximity.

CHAPTER 11

PROTECTIVE SAINTS

It is unsettling to spend multiple days with a large, intimidating man who does not speak to you at all. I experienced this years ago while hanging out with two Navy SEALs in Seattle.

One of them, who was a friend, rode in the passenger seat as I drove. We told stories and discussed various issues while the SEAL in the back sat in silence. This guy was huge, wore all black, and looked like he could decimate me in a moment. He wasn't coming across rude; it seemed he just had nothing to say. This dynamic continued throughout our weekend together—my friend and I interacted, and the other guy and I . . . didn't.

There came a moment, though, as we were driving along, when my buddy asked me if I had read a particular book. I said no, and my friend encouraged me to read it. It was a historical fiction book, which was not my typical genre, so I asked him why I should pick it up. For the first time all weekend, the man in the back spoke. To me. And he said these six words: "It is about the warrior mindset."

Now, let me tell you something: if a guy like that begins speaking after being silent for days, you are going to pay attention. Especially if you look at him and suddenly realize you've seen him before—on *Navy SEALs: BUDS Class 234*, a documentary about the process of becoming a SEAL.[1] You recall the episode on Hell Week, when candidates endure all the standard training challenges without the added comfort of sleep, and how at one point this guy in the back seat ran past the camera smiling. When *that* man recommends a book explaining how a warrior mindset works, you are going to pick it up, I promise you. I did.

It was indeed about the warrior mindset.

It was specifically about the Spartans—not the ones from Michigan State University, but the ancient Greek warrior culture.[2] While there is much to disregard about the Spartan way of life, they did have two things going for them.

First, they were an extraordinarily *focused* society. Their energies were almost entirely centralized on warfare. When young boys reached about kindergarten age, the men took them out into the fields to teach them how to fight. No elective classes. No humanities. Just tips on how to take out the enemy. They trained their young men in a form of combat they had mastered.

When the Spartans went to battle, it did not look like the movie *Braveheart*, where a mass of fighters gets fired up and charges into the fray. They instead would form up in ranks, press their shields into the backs of the men in front of them, and, when the signal was given, run forward together as one united army. This essentially made them into a massive human battering ram. When that singular column of warriors made contact with the enemy lines, they would plow right through them.

So if you were a Thessalonian or Athenian marshaled on the battlefield to fight and learned the Spartans were on the other side, you'd quickly put away the sword and shield you brought. You'd break out your pen and paper and start writing out your terms of surrender. You didn't mess with these guys. They had two things that made them unstoppable: focus and unity. Whenever you have a community that is focused and unified, you have a dangerous crew.

It was no wonder the guy in the back seat connected with this book. The SEALs are like the Spartans: they are focused men who travel in packs.

WE ARE LOST WITHOUT EACH OTHER

Do you know who else had focus and unity going for them? The early church. Luke described the first followers of Jesus as "devoted . . . to the apostles' teaching and the fellowship," and that combination made them a force in the world (Acts 2:42). One critic of the apostle Paul and his team said in exasperation, "These men . . . have turned the world upside down" (17:6). The world changes whenever a community possesses these two characteristics. They are meant to be essential, defining characteristics of the people of Jesus.

This prompted Paul to write his letter to the Philippians. He started out by calling them the "fellowship in the gospel" and "partakers . . . of grace" (1:5, 7 NKJV). He was confirming that they were God's people. How do you know that you are truly a Christian? You love Christ. How do you know if you are saved? You cherish the Savior. Paul saw in the Philippians the same fire he saw in himself. They were a focused people.

They just had one problem: they weren't unified. They had trouble getting along. Does that by chance sound familiar to you—the report of Christians not getting along? Yep, believers from centuries past experienced the same kind of friction we do today.

Sometimes our churches can be as cliquish and weird as our junior highs. Some of you have felt this, maybe even within yourself. A friend tells you that they are going to a different church in town and then proceeds to enumerate all the ways their church is amazing. Something inside you wants to say, "Yeah, I heard that place is great if you're into inauthentic worship. Good luck with that." We have trouble celebrating others!

Now, some may say, "That is so shameful. Not celebrating others. I can't imagine. I personally don't have any enemies. I mean, sure, there are people at work I can't stand and I secretly hope they fail in life. But enemies? Not a one."

If we are honest, we will admit that people get on our nerves. When I was in college, I had a friend who would consistently invite me to lunch and then "forget" his wallet. And, of course, it was always at places I could barely afford. I'd find myself locked into the situation for a couple hours because he chewed so incredibly slowly. No kidding, the man averaged thirty-two chews for every bite of food. How do I know this? Because I counted. And averaged. Everything in me wanted to scream, *Swallow, man! It's ready for the next phase of digestion!* We could all speak honestly about the fact that other people, even fellow believers in Jesus, can be a real hassle sometimes.

Yet Paul went so far as to say that believers would never reach their God-given potential without others. He explained to the Ephesians that God "gave some as apostles, some as prophets, some as evangelists, some as pastors and teachers, for the equipping of the saints . . . for the building up of the body of Christ; until we all attain to the unity of the faith, and . . . the measure of the stature which belongs to the fullness of Christ" (4:11–13 NASB).

Your full human potential cannot be achieved in isolation. True spirituality is always worked out in the context of community. We will never be complete in Christ without unity in the body of Christ. We can be focused. But we must also have unity.

Seven times in Genesis 1 God declared as he created, "It is good." In chapter 2 we see the first report of "not good": "It is not good that the man should be alone" (v. 18). What did God mean by "alone"? After all, Adam was with God. The perfect quiet time seven days a week. But God is community within himself: Father, Son, and Holy Spirit. The Godhead is a party, with all three members delighting in and rejoicing over the other. He is a unity of diversity. And we are meant to enjoy the same.

Our relentless commitment to individuality has created ever-increasing isolation in the world today, and we have been hurt by this. Loneliness abounds, and much of our struggle with anxiety comes from the lack of a community to help buffer us from life's disappointments. We are not meant to be cul-de-sacs of God's grace. We are meant to be conduits to one another.

Looking back at Philippians 1, after extolling the beauties of the gospel for several verses, Paul turned the corner and called the Philippians to action. He challenged them with one singular admonition: "Only conduct yourselves in a manner worthy of the gospel of Christ" (v. 27 NASB). What does that look like?

In Greek the words "conduct yourselves in a manner worthy" are all contained in a single term: *politeuesthe*. It is built off the word *polis*, which means "city." In a literal sense the term *politeuesthe* means "to live or discharge your obligations as a citizen of a city." Back then, the city you came from formed a core sense of your identity. You saw yourself in the context of a community. One novelist summarized it this way: "A man without a city is not a man."[3]

Paul used this word only with the Philippians, because he knew it

TRUE SPIRITUALITY IS ALWAYS WORKED OUT IN THE CONTEXT OF COMMUNITY.

would mean something to them. Of all Greeks they were particularly proud of their city. The city was a gift from the caesar to the soldiers who had fought bravely against the forces of Brutus and Cassius. And even though Philippi is far from Rome, the citizens were granted all the privileges of Roman citizenship. So for a Philippian, the idea of living up to the ideals of those who sacrificed in order to purchase you this new citizenship was a deeply treasured value.

Later in his letter Paul used the root word again, saying, "Our citizenship [*polituma*] is in heaven, and from it we await a Savior, the Lord Jesus Christ" (Philippians 3:20). The message was that these believers belonged to an eternal community purchased through the valiant effort of the greatest Rescuer who ever lived.

We do too. So let's live into what he valued. Let's embody what matters to him. Let's honor what he honors. What does that look like? What does a citizen of Christ's kingdom do?

Paul spelled it out for the Philippians like this: "Only let your manner of life be worthy of the gospel of Christ, so that whether I come and see you or am absent, I may hear of you that you are *standing firm in one spirit,* with *one mind striving side by side* for the faith of the gospel" (1:27).

WE STAND TOGETHER

One spirit. One mind. Standing together. Side by side, giving our lives together for that which matters most. We flee and pursue *together*—that is how we honor the King. We commit ourselves to the community he gave his life for.

Let's say you decided that you love me. What is the greatest thing you could do for me? That's easy—love my kids. Be kind to them.

Care about them. Do what is best for them. If you said to me, "Ben, I think you're great. But I can't stand your kids. I honestly cannot tolerate being around them. Get them away from me!" then I've got news for you—we probably aren't going to be friends. There is no separation between me and my kids. To love me is to love them, even if they're difficult at times.

God is building a glorious family. Jesus lived and died to purchase an "us"—a community of formerly hostile parties now knit together for his glory. Fight for this. Take up the enormous privilege—and at times extreme hassle—of being part of God's beloved community.

Listen, life is hard. We do not prioritize community only because it honors Jesus. We also do it because *we need us.*

We need a strong community so we can stand firm. Paul's terminology calls to mind imagery of a soldier's cleats dug into the dirt so they will offer resistance. We need the stability of community when we face the challenges that come our way.

The Spartan shield covered not only the one carrying it but the man next to him as well. If you were a typical soldier in those days, you might have had an impulse to lean toward the man next to you so you could enjoy maximum coverage from his shield. But doing this left the man on your other side with less coverage from *your* shield. In some armies, entire battle lines of men collapsed before the first clash of swords because some soldiers did this in self-preservation. The tragic irony was that it caused the compromise of the entire front and all but ensured their defeat.

The Spartans, however, would never do this. They deeply believed that their sword was for their enemy and their shield was for their brother. They would march toward whatever danger lay ahead with confidence because they knew they advanced together.

We need this kind of brotherhood if we are going to stand firm in the midst of the difficulties of life. We need each other in order to stand.

Some of us have been rendered combat ineffective because we run out into the battlefield of life alone. In the secret and quiet places of our lives, lust or insecurity ravages us. And as shame keeps us locked in isolation, our addictions sap us of our strength.

Maybe we rationalize our secrecy: *David fought Goliath alone. I can handle this problem alone too. I don't need to ask for help from anyone.* Yes, David did overpower Goliath on his own. But keep reading. Later we discover an occasion in battle when David became weary. In that moment another giant overpowered him and was about to kill him. The man had even brought a new sword for the occasion! David needed Abishai to step in front of him in order to save his life (2 Samuel 21:15–17).

We may be able to conquer our besetting sins alone for a night or two. Maybe even a whole week. But inevitably life will send us days where things do not go our way, and in the grind of existence, we become discouraged and tired.

Remember this: weariness + isolation = failure.

Some of us have lived in this cycle of defeat for years. Even decades. But there is a way out: God has given you a key to freedom. It is called "us."

Loneliness always lurks at our door. We must fight this powerful undercurrent pulling us toward isolation—not with a broad swath of a thousand friends, but with a few close, deep friendships. Even Jesus called for his friends to pray with him in his hour of greatest need. For some of you, the most Christlike thing you will do this year is start praying for a friend or two who will stand with you.

COMMUNAL EFFORT

Paul told Timothy to "flee youthful passions and pursue righteous-ness, faith, love, and peace, *along with those who call on the Lord from a pure heart*" (2 Timothy 2:22). Do you have a community to run with? A handful of people who want to chase after God as much as you do? One of God's greatest gifts to us is an "us" to lean on. We were never meant to run alone.

Many of us find ourselves repeating a predictable pattern of addic-tion. When we fail, we ask God for forgiveness, and the good news is, we receive it. When we confess, "he is faithful and just to forgive us our sins and to cleanse us from all unrighteousness" (1 John 1:9). But we find that we need more than just forgiveness; we need healing. We need that broken part of ourselves repaired.

God has provided a remedy in James 5:16: "Confess your sins to one another and pray for one another, that you may be healed." God's remedy for our repeated failure is community. In the con-text of other believers who sincerely desire to live with purity and integrity, we can find the strength to walk away from destructive patterns. They say in Alcoholics Anonymous, "We are only as sick as our secrets."[4]

When I was fresh out of college and new in ministry, I found that I was still struggling with some besetting sins that I just couldn't consistently conquer. So I went on a ruthless campaign in my own per-sonal life to eliminate all the moments where I gave in to temptation. But I still found that the right combination of sadness or weariness and opportunity led me to failure repeatedly.

One day as I was praying about this obvious pattern in my life, God brought that passage in James to mind. If I wanted to be healed,

I needed to confess to someone else. I could not beat this on my own. That was disappointing for me to admit. I wanted to believe I was strong enough to beat it on my own, but repeated failure told a different story.

I realized I was standing at a crossroads. I had to decide if I would be content with perceived holiness, or if I wanted practical holiness. Perceived holiness concerns itself with whether I look good in the eyes of other people. As long as sins are hidden from view, they are acceptable. Practical holiness says something different. It says I want integrity—a word that is built off the word *integer*, which means "one." I did not want to praise God in public and rebel against him in private. I wanted to be the same inside and out.

I needed to find someone who was pursuing God "from a pure heart," like Paul had described. I needed someone who wanted purity before God as much as I did. A dear friend came to mind. I'll be honest: I resisted the thought at first. It was important to me at the time that I looked impressive to this guy, and I knew confessing sin was going to change what he thought of me.

I was afraid of the risk.

But I was afraid of being a fake more and decided to give it a try.

I asked him if he would meet me in my office, and I confessed to him everything I was struggling with, even the sad little compromises. Afterward I felt very vulnerable.

As soon as I finished, he waited for a moment, then replied, "Well, here are mine." And he confessed his temptations and compromises to me as well.

When he finished I replied, "Wow. You are a sick person. You've got problems."

No. I'm kidding. In that moment we both felt a tremendous sense of relief. David said when he left his sin unconfessed it sapped his strength like the heat of summer (Psalm 32:3–4). It felt like we had both unshouldered a huge burden of guilt and shame off our backs. We felt lighter.

We both got on our knees in my office and prayed for each other. We continued to pray regularly for each other for years. This honesty, support, and unity reduced our addictive behavior, and in time we both experienced a level of freedom that, I'll be honest, hadn't seemed possible for most of my life. We also found that integrity felt good. There is a sense of agency and moral authority that lands in your chest when you realize you don't have to be owned by your desires.

I want that for you. But there is only one way to get it.

No one can experience freedom from persistent struggles on their own. And the great news is, you don't have to. God has given us an "us" so that with one mind we can stand.

SUPPORTIVE FRIENDS IN THE LIGHT

When I was a youth pastor, a young man confessed to me that he struggled with an addiction to pornography. I asked him to describe any pattern he saw in his relapses, and he answered: His computer. In his bedroom. Late at night. He couldn't stop.

I quoted Romans 13:14, the verse about making no provision for the flesh, and told him to eliminate the moment. "Get the computer out of your bedroom," I said.

"I can't," he replied. "My mom put it there. If she sees me carrying it out of my room, she'll ask me about it. What would I say? 'Just a little porn addiction, Mom!' I don't think I'm ready to have that conversation."

So he tried unplugging it. But then he would just plug it back in. He set new passwords. But then he would take them off.

As we continued to meet I decided to stop talking as much about the porn issue and turn our focus to the Word of God. We studied the beauties of what it was to love and be loved by God, to be a part of his family.

Then one day he came by my office unannounced. He held up his ethernet cable (back when we plugged these directly into our computers), then placed it on my desk. With a look of relief he said, "Here. It's not going to own me anymore."

The next day his best friend showed up at my office. He set his ethernet cable on my desk, too, and said, "Heard you're collecting these. See ya later."

These young men began to pray for each other and encourage each other. A year later the second largest constituency of students in our ministry came from their high school, which was not particularly near to our church. Why? It was not because they were hitting folks in the halls over the head with their Bibles. It was because people would tell them, "You seem different. Lighter. Happier." And they could confidently say, "God is changing my life." Sobriety had opened the door to ministry, and it would not have been possible without the support of a loving community.

Some of you are content to make an uneasy peace with ways of thinking and living that compromise your integrity. You may rationalize that these little daily compromises don't have that noticeable of an impact. But you have no idea what creativity, productivity, and spirituality could be released in your life when you begin to walk with a supportive community into the light.

Another young man confided in me that he wrestled deeply with depression. I encouraged him to tell some trusted friends. He hesitated. He felt a powerful sense of shame about his inability to make the darkness lift.

Later that year we both attended a retreat with a group of his high school peers. One night, after listening to a powerful lecture, we were sitting in our cabin talking about what we'd been learning. In that safe environment he took the brave step to share about his depression. He explained why he had missed so many days of school, that sometimes he felt so sad he could not get out of bed.

After a brief moment of silence, another young man spoke up, "I struggle like that too."

While this moment of honesty did not solve all of their problems, it did remove a painful sense of isolation. Sharing their concerns with a supportive community also helped them feel not so controlled by those concerns. Empathy helps dissolve shame.

They stayed connected to this community of young men and kept praying for one another.

About a year later the first young man was sitting next to me at church. With a few minutes left in the gathering, he got up to quietly slip out, as was his custom. On the way out the door he turned back and flashed a mischievous grin at me. He knew that I knew where he was going. He always left a bit early so he could drive around the neighborhood and pick up several of his friends from theater class and bring them to the next service. And he always flashed that smile at me because he knew it made me nervous how many kids he packed into his tiny car. I have always loved that quick interaction of ours because it signified his progress. Sure, he still battled depression, but that wasn't the dominant narrative of his life. He had a supportive community, and from that position of strength he was leveraging his life to help others.

Purity, liberty, and integrity are the fruits of vibrant community.

WE STRIVE TOGETHER

The Christian life isn't just about not getting dirty with the sin of the world though. We are not just playing defense. We avoid destruction so we can accomplish our God-given mission and do good in the world! We need community to do this as well. We want to live united, "with one mind striving side by side for the faith of the gospel" (Philippians 1:27).

We strive together. Not against each other, but on the same team, striving together for the same ultimate goal.

But we can get that mixed up sometimes, can't we?

Several years ago a buddy of mine invited me over to play a new military-style video game that his company had developed. The gist of the game was that we were to work as a team to rescue some hostages. At one point when I moved my character forward, my controls suddenly went dead. "I think your game is glitchy," I said.

"No," my buddy replied, "I think I just shot you in the back of the head."

Well. We are never going to accomplish our mission if we keep taking shots at each other, are we?

Sometimes we are great with having friends just as long as we excel past them in areas we deem important. As long as I'm more athletic, or attractive, or popular, or fashionable, or successful, I will be your friend. We impede our ability to work together as a team because we are too focused on our individual stats. We are meant to struggle, not against each other, but alongside each other!

Paul spoke of striving together for the faith of the gospel. We work together to get this message out. We need one another to do it.

We need community to challenge one another, to sharpen one another, and to spur one another on toward love and good deeds. We need great minds helping us understand the more complex elements of our faith. We need women and men with pastoral gifts and counseling skills to help us navigate our own deep emotional waters. We need great organizers to rally us to accomplish grander goals than any of us could tackle on our own. *We need us.*

When I was in college a young woman I knew wanted to host a car wash. I asked her what organization we would be doing it for. She said, "No organization."

I responded, "Well, then who would people donate money to?"

She said we would not be taking any donations.

"Then why are we doing this?" I asked.

"We will tell people, 'Christ came not to be served, but to serve, so we wanted to do the same,'" she explained.

Okay. I thought it sounded kinda strange, but I was willing to go for it.

She was an organized girl, but not the most vocal. A few of us were more gifted at rallying the people. So we spread the vision with some friends and she organized the parking lot, the hoses, the buckets. She even planned the whole layout of the day: A few of us would wash cars. A few would cook hot dogs. Another group would be available to have conversations with people as they waited to get their cars back.

I was on wheel duty. As I cleaned the hubcaps of a vehicle, the owner approached me. "So what organization is this car wash for?"

"No organization."

"Then who do I give the money to?"

"We're not taking money."

"Then why are you doing this?"

"Great question." I quoted my friend: "We're Christians, and Christ came not to be served but to serve. So we wanted to serve people today."

I'll never forget his response. He shouted, "No!" It was not at all what I expected. He sat down on the curb next to me and began to cry.

He explained that he had been out of work for months. He'd exhausted all his options and had begun to lose hope. That morning he'd decided to head out and get drunk. When he saw the car wash, he figured he'd turn in and get the car cleaned so that when he came home his wife might be a little less mad.

He then buried his face in his hands and cried more. He kept repeating, "I just can't believe y'all are doing this." I was able to place a hand on his shoulder and pray for this man at this crucial moment in his life. It was one of the more meaningful moments of my college career, and I would not have been out there if it hadn't been for my quiet but determined friend. We need *us* to be fully who we are meant to be.

You may be thinking, *Ben, this all sounds great, but what if I don't have friends like this? What if my community doesn't feel like this?* Let me encourage you: stay focused, and ask God to bring unity.

As I mentioned earlier, David did have to face Goliath alone. But he made the choice. Even if no one else wanted to walk by faith, he would. He stepped onto the battlefield alone, and the Scriptures record two different responses in the crowd.

Saul, the king, became jealous of David. The songs about David's victory made him "very angry" (1 Samuel 18:8). You may see something similar happen. Maybe some of your friends won't want to hang with you if you choose to walk with God.

Jonathan, Saul's son, had an entirely different response. He had done something just as brave and crazy as David just a few chapters before—he faced off against the Philistines alone! When he saw David walk by faith, it stirred his heart of faith. First Samuel 18:1 records, "The soul of Jonathan was knit to the soul of David, and Jonathan loved him as his own soul." Jonathan started giving David stuff—his own robe, his armor, his credit card. He was just so excited to find someone who wanted to run after God as much as he did. And when David hit some of the toughest challenges in his life in the days ahead, Jonathan "strengthened his hand in God" (1 Samuel 23:16).

Make the decision today that you will flee youthful lusts and pursue righteousness, joy, and peace, and you will begin to see to your right and to your left those who are running alongside you with a pure heart. Join a church in your community and get involved. Volunteer and watch friendships form as you serve shoulder-to-shoulder in God's work. In my time as pastor of Passion City Church, Washington, DC, I have seen time and again deep friendships form among those who initially arrived at church alone. It has been one of my greatest joys in life to watch those friends be there for one another to celebrate the highs and mourn the lows together. I believe the same can happen for you, if you are willing to bravely take the first step. I am cheering you on all the way!

RHYTHMS OF REST

1. Take a moment and ask God to bring to mind a mature believer in Jesus you could stand with through the trials of life. What might it look like for you to ask them to pray for you and for you to offer to do the same for them?
2. Ask yourself where you see brothers and sisters in Jesus striving together to do good in your community. Consider praying for the courage to run alongside them in the work!

CHAPTER 12

POSITIVE RELEASE

Several years ago while Donna and I were sitting at a coffee shop, a young man snatched my wife's iPhone off the table right in front of us. Ever wonder how you'd react in such a situation? My wife instinctively yelled, "Get 'em, babe!"

What other choice did I have as a husband but to kick off my sandals and race after him?

I turned the corner and saw a vehicle marked Security. I called out for help, until I realized that the security car was driven by his friend—it was their getaway car! I grabbed the door, and his buddy hit the gas. So we took off down the street together, with me hanging from the passenger-side door.

These boys were the same age as the high school students I had been preaching to all week. So while I was hanging from the car door, I was talking softly to them, telling them they didn't want to do this. They were calling me "sir." It was all a bit surreal.

I realized I had only two options: either jump in the car with them and escalate this situation, or simply let go. When they slowed for a moment I released my grip on the car and tumbled to a stop on the pavement. They drove maybe a hundred more yards before being intercepted by the police.

I reconnected with Donna and, as the adrenaline began to subside in my body, I turned to her and said, "My back hurts." It hurt a little more the following day. Then on the third day, I woke up in excruciating pain and was unable to stand. Several doctor visits and an MRI later, I discovered that I had two bulging discs and one herniated disc in my lower back. The worst of them was sticking out almost three centimeters and pressing on a nerve that sent waves of unrelenting pain down my leg.

Multiple doctors indicated that I needed surgery right away. But the surgeon refused, explaining it would be too risky because of my past back injuries, as well as a previous spinal surgery. He added that something had to change soon or I might lose the use of my right foot.

I asked if he could just hurry up and fix it because I was about to enter a busy season of ministry.

He said, "I need to acclimate you to your new reality." He then pointed at my pregnant wife. "You can't help her. You won't be able to hold that baby. I am not even sure at this point that you will be able to walk again." This is when it felt like the room began to spin.

His best solution for me? "Go home and hope your back heals itself."

So I went home and lay facedown on the floor in my living room for a month. The medications made me feel sick, so I ate little and dropped forty pounds. The prescribed steroids gave me insomnia, so I slept only a few hours a night. To cope, I watched movies—hundreds of movies. It got so bad that one night I even watched *Teen Wolf Too* starring Jason Bateman. I thought, *This is pathetic. I'm so sick of watching movies. But what other option do I have? Sit here alone with my thoughts?*

I turned the TV off. And in that moment I felt like God whispered to me in that gentle but convicting voice, *Are you ready to talk to me now?* I realized I had been filling my life with distractions so that I wouldn't have to deal with the big issues right in front of me. And, if I was really honest, it hadn't been only in this moment on the floor that I had done it.

Slowly, gently, over the course of days, the Lord began to give me the gift that is far too lacking in the world today: reflection. A time to process. I came to realize that over the course of several years I had been living a life where I constantly toggled between pursuing relentless ambition and slumping into numbing distraction. Suddenly I had a month on my face to be still before the Lord. To wait patiently on him because there was literally nothing else I could physically do.

My mind drifted to Psalm 23 in which David declared that the Lord was his shepherd. "He makes me lie down in green pastures. He leads me beside still waters. He restores my soul" (vv. 2–3). I had never thought of that line "he makes me lie down" as a particularly violent image, but I realized that my relentless pace was so destructive that God, in his mercy, had forced me to lie down so he could restore my soul.

There is much I learned in that season, but one lesson stands out in my mind now: committed Christians—even those in ministry positions—are prone to break.

Some break morally. I had watched a man who taught me about the grace of God leave his wife and kids to run away with his lover. I had seen within my first five years of ministry five men I knew personally exit the ministry due to infidelity. Others break emotionally. I had also seen mentors of mine who had maintained a high moral standard begin to show signs of emotional strain. Suddenly their joy was gone. Hope had fled. And it took a long time for them to feel normal again.

As I lay there on the floor, it became apparent to me that I had not considered how I might break physically. I had stored up years of anxiety in my body, and the body keeps score.[1] The longer my rehabilitation lasted, the more I discovered that I was a time bomb about to go off. I clocked in long hours of bad posture at a desk. I would miss a few days of workouts because of work, then head to the gym and try to attack a session at full tilt to make up for lost time. I wasn't listening to my body when it hurt or when headaches came on. I just kept pushing myself—unknowingly to a breaking point. No, I didn't break morally or emotionally, but boy did I break physically. I realized that to go forward, I had to adapt to a new rhythm of life by both attacking problems and embracing restorative rest.

THE OUTER RING

In this season of life, I also began a friendship with a man who would become an invaluable mentor. Growing up in a difficult environment, he had turned to sex as an escape from emotional pain. When life had become unmanageable, he'd checked in at an inpatient treatment center for sexual addiction. I became friends with him years after that point, when he was living a healthy life of sobriety. I found his rigorous honesty refreshing. He had the settled temperament of a man who had fought a long war and was enjoying a hard-won peace.

In one of our many conversations, he shared with me a worksheet he had used while in treatment that was transformative for him. It looked like a simple target with a bull's-eye in the middle and two large rings around it. Inside the bull's-eye he had written every activity that constituted a breach of his sobriety. Activities that, if he engaged in them, would set the count of days of sobriety back to zero.

Admittedly he used to love doing everything in that circle, and part of him would still love to do them. But he had lived enough life to know the damage that path would bring, both to himself and his loved ones. He knew that whisper of sweet release was a lie. He never wanted to enter that circle again.

In the ring just outside the bull's-eye, he had written all the behaviors that, for him, were usually indicators that he was headed toward relapse. They were actions that, though not a breach of sobriety, flirted with the line. Some of them sounded like things that would be completely harmless to others. But he knew once he started down this path, it inevitably led toward the inner circle. This was the ring of temptation.

He never wanted to enter this ring again either. Whenever the activities in this ring started to make sense to him or sound attractive, he knew he should immediately call a friend. He needed another voice to interrupt and contradict the one in his head that said these little compromises would be harmless. He'd been fooled too many times before to believe it again.

As my friend was explaining the first two rings on his worksheet, I found myself wondering about the third, outer ring. *Was it the things you do* before *those indicators that you were about to violate your sobriety?* That seemed a bit extreme.

When I asked, "What's the outer ring?" he answered, "These are the things I do for fun. The things I enjoy. The stuff that brings life to me without asking for a soul-crushing compromise. The third ring contains the activities that are soul restorative for me."

He said he'd been surprised at how hard it was for him to write that list, and it was that very exercise that helped him see the extent of the damage of his addiction. He'd been so sure that he had to act out in inappropriate ways to have fun, convinced they were the only places he could be happy. What he did not realize was that they were keeping him from a whole world of beautiful, simple pleasures that had no sorrow added to them.

Then he challenged me to get my own worksheet and fill out the three rings. I did my best. I felt I had a better-than-average grasp on my besetting sins and the triggering activities that led to them. I felt pretty solid about the bull's-eye and the inner ring.

When I got to that outer ring, though, I was completely stumped. I think I wrote, "read books."

He pressed me here, saying, "I don't want to talk about these inner rings at all. I want you to notice how sad and pathetic your outer ring is. You do not even know what you enjoy doing."

He was absolutely right. I didn't know how to have fun. I had to fix this.

I imagine that today you may need to fix this as well. And not just so you can be a more relaxed, enjoyable person, as wonderful as that would be. You need to fix this because that outer ring is one of your best defenses against the inner two rings.

Let me tell you something disturbing about yourself: when your marriage or your ministry or your career or your friends cease to be fun, you will seek pleasure somewhere else. We are pleasure-seeking machines. And if you do not actively observe what your positive releases are and prioritize them, you'll be more vulnerable to the Enemy's suggestions. Your self-discipline may keep you from certain sins for a time, but when you are tired, frustrated, or feel a sense of entitlement, the Enemy will solicit your mind with illicit alternatives, and you will be primed for a fall. Or, he will encourage you to keep your foot on the gas (like I did), and then you will break something either in your body or in your soul.

This is why it's so important that you find positive places to take your need to unwind.

Again, David said in Psalm 23, "The LORD is my shepherd; I shall not want. He makes me lie down in green pastures. He leads me beside still waters. He restores my soul" (vv. 1–3). If your rhythm of life never involves soul-restorative rest, lying down in green pastures and beside cool waters, then you need to be honest with yourself that God is not shepherding your life. You are being led along by something else: your fears, your ego, your ambitions, your need to be validated, or your lusts.

When God is guiding your life, you may have seasons when you go hard. There were times when Jesus worked all day and all night! But those times will always be coupled with times of restorative rest. And if you lack those times, you will break.

JESUS HAD RHYTHM

You see this rhythm throughout Jesus' ministry. Even a casual observer will see that Christ adopted a rhythm of rest and war. He would enter a city for intense ministry, then exit to the wilderness for solitude and rest.

Mark described a single day in which Jesus preached, cast out a demon, and healed late into the night all the people who had followed him home—they were so packed into Peter's house, they were breaking down the door. Then Mark, whose writing style was fast-paced, slowed down his language: "Rising very early in the morning, while it was still dark, he departed and went out to a desolate place, and there he prayed" (Mark 1:35).

Jesus switched gears. You can see him do this over and over again, particularly at key moments. He had three years of ministry in which to change the entire world. Yet that calling never made him abandon the rhythm of rest.

He taught this rhythm to his disciples as well: "He appointed twelve (whom he also named apostles) so that they might be with him and he might send them out to preach and have authority to cast out demons" (Mark 3:14–15). Their first job was to be with him. Just to orbit Jesus' life and soak up his vision and his values. Then Jesus empowered them and released them to do the very things he had been doing: preach and cast out demons.

When he first sent them out to do this they returned to him amped! They were not exhausted or depleted. They were energized by their ministry success. So they might have been surprised when Jesus said to them, "Come away by yourselves to a desolate place and rest a while." Mark then explained, "For many were coming and going, and they had no leisure even to eat" (Mark 6:31).

Health experts tell us that if you wait until you're thirsty to drink water, then you're already dehydrated. Here Jesus showed us that if you wait until you are completely exhausted to rest, then you are already in trouble. Rest is meant to be a rhythm. God wove this pattern into creation.

CREATION AND RECREATION

In six days God created the entire world and on the seventh day he rested. Not because he was tired; he doesn't get tired. What he had made was good, so he set aside a day to pull back and just enjoy it. This coincided with the first full day of human existence. Our God wanted us to rest and enjoy before any work even started. He created us to enjoy him, and that involves enjoying what he has made.

A word we often use for fun is *recreation*. Think about that as re-creation. To grow again. To refresh by way of fun. Faith-filled fun is fundamental to survival. You need it.

If you do not prioritize a redemptive release, the Enemy will always be there to offer a destructive one. You must consciously choose redemptive fun or you will slouch toward destructive fun. It is a guarantee. There is no middle ground. For the sake of our souls, we must rediscover the ancient path of having fun!

When God carved out a place on this planet for our first parents, he named it Eden—which, as I've mentioned before, means "delight." He didn't just make their abode functional; he made it awesome! He made it "pleasant to the sight and good for food" (Genesis 2:9). Did you notice the order of his priorities there? Before he made it functional, he made it beautiful. He wanted it to look amazing. He wanted his people to be dazzled by beauty.

God is not a killjoy—he *created* joy!

The Westminster Shorter Catechism states that "the chief end of man is to glorify God and enjoy Him forever."[2] And again, God designed us to enjoy him by enjoying what he has made.

For example, you glorify God in your eating when you enjoy the amazing flavors he's made. You honor him by delighting in his food and then thanking him that he didn't make the necessary act of fueling our bodies just an exercise in efficiency. He made it fun. He made it taste good.

God wove rest and enjoyment into the fabric of creation. And one of the ways we worship him is by embracing this rhythm of rest and restoration.

MAKE A JOYFUL NOISE

During the years I was a youth pastor I would take our interns out to Big Bend National Park in the wilderness of West Texas. It is a

IF YOU DON'T PRIORITIZE A REDEMPTIVE RELEASE, THE ENEMY WILL OFFER A DESTRUCTIVE ONE.

designated dark-sky zone, one of the few places on earth with almost no artificial light. The stars are so bright that they stop people in their tracks. These interns would literally shout for joy. "Look at that! You can see the whole Milky Way! The North Star is like a headlight! This is crazy!" The stars are big and bright deep in the heart of Texas, and these young people had never stopped to look up and enjoy them.

At one point we were driving into the depths of a canyon and listening to a worship song, one that talked about creation crying out in praise to God, and how we, his people, would join in and praise him too. I looked in the rearview mirror and the interns were crying. God's stunning creation had made their hearts ache, reaching a deep longing for beauty he had put inside them.

When was the last time you did that? Nothing is holding you back but you. We spend hours upon hours staring into screens, knowing they produce a sense of isolation, depression, anger, and anxiety. We keep doing it because we think we are supposed to. Take control of your life. Prioritize soul-restoring rest. In the name of Jesus, enjoy the world he made and thank him the whole time you're doing it.

What brings you joy? What makes you laugh? What makes your eyes light up? What do you look forward to? What do you check the calendar for again and again to make sure it's still there because you just can't wait to experience it? If you aren't living like this at some level, then you are completely missing out on how God intended life to be lived.

I COMMAND YOU TO CHILL

When God led his people triumphantly out of slavery in Egypt, he commanded them to weave rest into their rhythms. He designed multiple family, neighborhood, and nationwide barbecues (Deuteronomy 12:15–19; 16:11–15). No kidding! He wanted his people to just drop everything, grill up something, and chill, and make that kind of thing a regular part of their lives. He didn't only tell them to take the weekly Sabbath day off. He also gave them seasonal feasts and festivals and even whole years when they were meant to give the ground a break and not farm it! God was all about rest.

But it quickly got to a point where he had to demand that they take a day off. They repeatedly ditched the feast and festival days in order to keep working to make another dollar. They blew off the Sabbath years of rest so they could keep at the grind and get that extra paycheck. In fact, when the people of Judah were carried off into slavery in Babylon, God told them, "Now the land will get that Sabbath rest you refused to give it" (paraphrase of Leviticus 26:33–35).

This is what happened to me. I refused to take a day off every week. I kept working on holidays. I pushed crazy hours. Eventually, inevitably, I snapped because I was wound too tight. I broke because I was not loose. When I hit the ground I realized I had been functioning in an unhealthy manner for far too long. Your body will get the time off it needs. Either it will be in a healthy rhythm of rest, or in a hospital or rehabilitation facility. You decide how those hours will be doled out. By God's grace I'm trying to get the healthy rhythm right now.

REDISCOVERING RECREATION

As with my weekly and monthly rhythms, I give myself permission to regularly evaluate and recalibrate my list of positive releases. As life changes, so do we. Our interests vary and our options do as well.

Before we started a family, Donna and I loved finding ways to travel overseas. That became harder with babies, so we started taking more local trips instead. When the COVID-19 shutdown occurred, excursions were even harder to come by, so we started exploring hiking trails all around the DC area. The principle remains even as our opportunities and interests change; we may just apply it differently.

It took me awhile, but I found some things that are soul restorative for me, and then I developed habits that help me keep to the rhythm of rest:

- I often go on a walk in the woods first thing every morning. It's mild exercise and a great time to focus and pray, and it provides a much-needed break from hours of looking at a screen.
- I end most workdays with a phone call that is not so much a to-do-list, logistical call, but a fun, touch-base, encouragement one. I call a pastor friend to check in on them, or someone I've mentored or been mentored by to get an update. It's nice to end the workday with a call I look forward to all day.
- I always like to have a fun trip planned for sometime in the future. I've found even if it's six months away, just knowing it is out there lifts me up. I have a group of dear friends that annually tries to go off the grid and just hike and hang out together— that's an example of what I'm talking about here.
- I go on weekly adventures with my kids. Every Saturday we try to find and do some cool thing we've never experienced. Even if it's just an hour a day, the search for adventure is something we look forward to. We always make great memories and get to spend quality time together.
- I stay away from my phone on the weekend. I find that a day of reading an actual physical book I hold in my hands makes me feel good when I'm done.

- I always have one or two books I'm reading that aren't directly work related. They often end up being sermon illustrations, but that's not why I read them. I read them because they're fun. I choose a book because I'm interested in the subject and I like the style of the writing. For me, topics range from survival skills to fighting, to historical figures, to the occasional novel. Constantly learning something new keeps the mind sharp and gives me more opportunities for engaging with others in conversation.

- Donna and I sit on the back porch and visit at the end of each day. When something of note happens during the day, I know I can look forward to processing it together.

- I enjoy working out. Exercise releases endorphins, relieves stress, increases energy, and helps to avoid illness. We need all of that. The body works best when we make it work. After my back injury my doctor told me I could no longer run or lift weights, two things I really enjoyed. How do you work out without doing those two things? People pointed me to yoga, but I found it intensely boring. So I got into a whole world of gymnastics and bodyweight training literature. I found that learning a new skill while exercising is fun for me. I approached it like a student and it became more interesting.

What would it be for you?

I have friends who love cycling, playing basketball, and gardening. I don't like any of those things. Donna likes to write music and build things with her hands and cook. I don't like to do those things and don't want to learn how! I'm perfectly okay with that. The whole point here is to find out what each of us genuinely enjoys.

Some people like vacations where they sit at the beach and read a book. Honestly, that makes me feel stir-crazy. I like vacations that are a bit more active, when I can get out and explore wild places. I need an activity that engages my mind so it does not drift back to work. Neither kind of vacation is wrong; both serve a vital function. You need to retreat to go forward. You need to rest so you can run.

Boxing, golfing, surfing, hiking, biking, sailing, reading, walking, skydiving, skiing, hunting, swimming, flying, shooting, gardening, fishing, cooking, cleaning, touring, building, tinkering, camping, antiquing, sewing—whatever it might be, find the thing that makes you say, "Y'know, life is pretty great."

HISTORICAL FUN

Some of our deepest pain can be assuaged and darkest addictions avoided by prioritizing God-glorifying fun.

William Wilberforce was a force for good in the 1800s, leading the charge in Parliament to end slavery in Great Britain. This Herculean task absorbed most of his life. He was also a man who experienced severe physical pain. One of the critical components of his sustaining power throughout his life was his unbounded joy. A friend of his once remarked, "His presence was as fatal to dullness as to immorality. His mirth was as irresistible as the first laughter of childhood."[3] Fun fueled him so he could continue on his mission.

Martin Luther liked to bowl and to listen to great music. He also found his wife's keen sense of humor kept him afloat during his bouts of depression. He once wrote to a struggling younger saint, "Shun solitude. 'Eve got into trouble when she walked in the garden alone. I have my worst temptations when I am by myself.' Seek out some Christian brother, some wise counselor. Undergird yourself with the fellowship of the church. Then, too, seek convivial company . . . dine, dance, joke, and sing."[4]

Charles Spurgeon prioritized holidays at the sea. He urged his students, "It is wisdom to take occasional furlough. In the long run, we shall do more by sometimes doing less."[5]

He also wrote this description of how resting in nature affects human well-being (it's long, but it's good, I promise):

> He who forgets the humming of the bees among the heather, the coo-ing of the wood-pigeons in the forest, the song of birds in the woods, the rippling of rills among the rushes, and the sighing of the wind among the pines, needs not wonder if his heart forgets to sing and his soul grows heavy. A day's breathing of fresh air upon the hills, or a few hours' ramble in the beech woods' umbrageous calm, would sweep the cobwebs out of the brain of scores of our toiling ministers who are now but half alive. A mouthful of sea air, or a stiff walk in the wind's face, would not give grace to the soul, but it would yield oxygen to the body, which is the next best. . . . The ferns and the rabbits, the streams and the trouts, the fir trees and the squirrels, the primroses and the violets, the farm-yard, the new-mown hay, and the fragrant hops—these are the best medicine for hypochondri-acs, the surest tonic for the declining, the best refreshments for the weary. For lack of opportunity, or inclination, these great remedies are neglected, and the student becomes a self-immolated victim.[6]

In case you haven't used the word *self-immolated* yet today, I'll mention that it means doing harm to yourself. Spurgeon had a beauti-ful way of saying, "Go outside to be less sad."

Jonathan Edwards, who would frequently take horseback rides through the woods, wrote in his famous resolutions:

1. Resolved, That I will do whatsoever I think to be most to the glory of God, and my own good, profit, and pleasure, in the whole of my duration; without any consideration of the time, whether now, or never so many myriads of ages hence. . . .

2. Resolved, To be continually endeavouring to find out some new contrivance and invention to promote the forementioned things. . . .

3. Resolved, To live with all my might, while I do live.[7]

I'm with Edwards here. While I'm alive, I want to live with all my might. So I'm going to keep inviting God to fuel and restore my soul by following the rhythms of rest he has designed for us. How about you?

• • •

I will close this chapter by challenging you the same way my mentor challenged me. Draw a bull's-eye with three rings. In the inner ring write out the ways of thinking and living that you must never do again. They cost too much of your soul. In the middle ring write out the activities that always lead you to those integrity-compromising activities in the inner ring. In the outer ring write out what brings you soul-restoring rest. What do you do for fun? What makes your soul come alive? What brings you legitimate pleasure without compromising your integrity? Make a list.

Many people I have challenged to do this can't even write out three things they truly enjoy. If that's you, take a moment to grieve over how deceived you've been. Lament the loss. Then wipe away the tears and get to work on that list. Ask God to show you how to delight in him by delighting in what he has made.

Make the list at least twenty things. It may take you days to do this. That's okay. You may have to call some people and ask, "What do I like to do? When was the last time you saw me truly happy? When was the last time I laughed so hard my sides hurt? When was the last time I cried because of beauty?" Keep working. Make this a priority.

Next, pull out your calendar and ask yourself, "What three things will I incorporate into this week?" Start with the small ones. Then look out over the next three to six months and pick a bigger thing. Something that may require a little bit of planning. Then look at the next year or two and pick an even bigger one. Hike a national park. Go see Europe. Find your way to Jamaica and swim in the Blue Lagoon.

Rest in a way that fits you. Find your thing and actually do it. For the sake of God and everyone you influence, go on an adventure.

RHYTHMS OF REST

Once you've completed the exercise at the end of this chapter take some time to . . .

1. Write Psalm 23:1–3 and 6 in your journal, and meditate on it each day this week.
2. Dream about some soul-restoring, fun activities you've never done but would like to.
3. Articulate what this phrase means to you: "While I'm alive, I want to live with all my might."

CHAPTER 13

THE STORY OF THE SPIRIT

Years ago I spoke at an event at a university located on top of Lookout Mountain, Georgia. Donna and I discovered that the other side of the mountain was a popular hang-gliding spot, so we drove over and checked it out. As we watched people leap off the top of this mountain, we learned that beginners could drive to the base of the mountain and give it a shot.

So that's what we did.

Newbies were paired up with instructors, and before I knew it, my instructor and I were strapped into a sort of sleeping bag underneath a glider. Then we were wheeled out to an open field and hooked with a cable to the back of something I can only describe as a motorcycle with some wings glued on it. I confess that at that point I questioned whether this was a wise choice of entertainment.

My instructor said, "Okay, Bobby up there is going to pull us up into the air and then release us to hang glide."

Bobby is going to pull us up . . . with that? Is he, though?

Amazingly, everything happened just as he described. Bobby took off, and we went trailing after him.

The wind resistance was insane. We were winging about and shaking so violently that I felt like I was about to lose my breakfast any second. Right as I was prepared to hurl, Bobby released the cable . . . and we were one with the sky.

It was so peaceful. We floated gently above the earth. We communed with the birds. It was beautiful. Then the instructor began to turn us in circles, and we went up and up and up until the cars looked like tiny dots beneath us. When I asked him how we'd reached such an incredible elevation so quickly, he explained that we'd caught a thermal, an upward current of warm air.

If you jump off any old cliff under a glider, you'll (hopefully) just float down to the earth. But if there is a thermal, warm air rushes through a valley and up the side of a mountain, throwing air upward. If you've positioned yourself properly, you can catch that thermal and soar.

This is a picture of what it's like to experience true spirituality—to be united with the Spirit of God and live in the power only he can give.

IS THERE MORE?

We all want to be connected to something beyond ourselves that can take us farther than we can reach on our own. That's why there is so much interest in spirituality. We all feel the lack, the void, the sense that we are missing something. So we try to tap into something bigger than ourselves.

If you look at the statistics, almost everyone wants to be spiritual. In 2017 Pew Research conducted a poll in the US: 48 percent said they were *both* religious and spiritual; 27 percent said they were spiritual *but not religious*; and 6 percent said they were religious *but not spiritual*.[1] That means eight out of ten people in the US said they wanted some connection with the spiritual world—something greater than themselves they could be connected to and empowered by to live a better life.

The problem is, lots of people are confused about what that really means.

If you google the word *spiritual*, one of the first responses is the definition "relating to religion or religious belief." But, just like we saw in the Pew Research, some people view spirituality and religion as entirely separate. One *Psychology Today* article explained that spirituality means something different to everyone.[2] That is not helpful. If a word has a different meaning to everybody, then that word is objectively meaningless. If I want a donut and you hand me a salamander, we have miscommunicated. If you respond, "Well, this is what a donut is to me," I still need us to get on the same page before I'm able to enjoy a heavenly fried circle of dough.

I would submit that to be truly spiritual is *to be rightly related to the Spirit of God.* The good news is, God wants us to have communion with his Spirit. Jesus went so far as to say it was to his disciples' advantage that he go away, so he could send the Helper to them (John 16:7).

The Scriptures tell us that having this powerful, spiritual connection is the best way to live. "Look carefully then how you walk, not as unwise but as wise, making the best use of the time, because the days are evil. Therefore do not be foolish, but understand what the will of the Lord is. And do not get drunk with wine, for that is debauchery, but be filled with the Spirit" (Ephesians 5:15–18).

Your longing for spirituality is not silly or misplaced. It is because you are meant to be rightly related to the Spirit of God. You were made to fly—not simply be dragged through life as my hang glider was pulled by Bobby. We all would love to soar over obstacles, to experience an increase in the power and quality of our lives. We were meant for more than what we have now.

To help you better understand what it means to be spiritual, I want to tell you the story of the Spirit we find in Scripture. Then, in the next chapter, we'll work out the implications for our lives and what it means to walk by the Spirit.

The story of the Spirit begins with language. In Hebrew the word for "wind" is *ruach*. It became the word for "breath" as well, because your breath is your own personal wind. Then it also became the word for "spirit," because when someone died their spirit was gone.[3] How did they know? They didn't check their pulse back then; they leaned in to check their breathing. No breath? No wind? Then no spirit. They're dead. So wind, breath, and spirit are all translated from the same Hebrew word—*ruach*—and the Old Testament authors often played with that imagery.

THE INTIMACY OF THE
SPIRIT WITH CREATION

Genesis 1:2 states, "The earth was without form and void, and darkness was over the face of the deep. And the Spirit of God was hovering over the face of the waters."

The same word translated here as "hovering" is used in Deuteronomy 32:11, where it compares God's care of his beloved people to an eagle hovering over her young, spreading her wings over them in protection and carrying them with her pinions. It is a tender word. The Spirit of God is intimate with creation.

When it came time to make man, "The LORD God formed the man of dust from the ground and breathed into his nostrils the breath of life, and the man became a living creature" (Genesis 2:7). Do you hear the *intimacy* in that? He breathed his breath into Adam's nostrils. He didn't do that with the cows.

Have you ever had someone breathe on you? They need to be close for you to feel that. This was such an intimate scene; God was not a distant deity in Genesis.

Don't miss the poetry of the description either. What was man made of? He was dust and the wind of God. This helps us understand the role of God's Spirit: he is the intimate, animating presence of God.

Then, out of pride, humanity rebelled against God. It was not so much that Adam and Eve broke a rule as it was that they violated a relationship. From there the curse ensued. As Paul described it, "Their foolish hearts were darkened" (Romans 1:21). The light went out inside of them. They died spiritually.

God said to Adam, "By the sweat of your face you shall eat bread, till you return to the ground, for out of it you were taken; for you are dust, and to dust you shall return" (Genesis 3:19).

Remember, man was made from dust and the wind of God. What was missing after the fall? The wind. Man was still alive, but the intimate, animating presence of God was no longer close. Humanity's guilt broke the bond, and as a result, Adam and Eve felt lost and powerless.

And we feel it to this day, as we walk the road Adam and Eve walked. Novelist Thomas Wolfe described it this way:

> The whole conviction of my life now rests upon the belief that the
> sense of loneliness far from being a rare and curious phenomenon
> peculiar to myself and a few other solitary people is the central and

inevitable fact of human existence. All this hideous doubt, despair and dark confusion of the soul a lonely person must know. . . . He has no faith in him except his own and often that faith deserts him and leaves him shaken and filled with impotence.[4]

Chapter 5 of Genesis drives this terrible fact home, as eight times throughout the genealogy it repeats the refrain, "and he died . . . and he died . . . and he died." We are alive, but the wind is gone. As the story of God's people in the Old Testament unfolds, we see not only a lack of God's intimate presence, we also see a lack of his power.

FIXING OUR HEART PROBLEM

In time God forged his covenant people and gave them the law through his servant Moses. Jesus summarized this law in two critical commands: to love the Lord your God with all your heart, soul, and mind, and to love your neighbor as yourself (Matthew 22:37–40). The whole law of God unpacks various ways and means to love God and each other. Yet it becomes painfully apparent that the people of God sometimes do right, but mostly do wrong. And, in the end, they appear wholly incapable of following the laws of God.

God predicted this. When the law was first given to the people, they threw a party and declared to Moses, "All the words which the Lord has spoken we will do!" When God heard this, he responded with, "If only they had such a heart in them" (Exodus 24:3; Deuteronomy 5:29 NASB). Kind of a buzzkill, honestly. They wanted to try to do everything right, but God told them they didn't have the tools to do it.

These laws were not horribly oppressive. Read Leviticus and Numbers. If you were starting a nation from scratch on a deserted island, you could do a whole lot worse. Don't kill each other. Don't take things that belong to others. If someone loses a donkey and you find it, give it back to them. Don't lie in court. Take a day off every seventh day. The law sets the guidelines for a community that should treat one another with respect and love.

But they simply couldn't keep the law. The pull of selfishness was too strong. The law was not the problem; there was something deeply flawed in people! They knew the good they ought to do, yet they remained powerless to do it.

After a few hundred years of demonstrable failure, God reiterated his solution. One day a hero would come, and he would bring the wind with him.

Isaiah said that "the Spirit of the LORD shall rest upon him" (Isaiah 11:2). There would be a time when God's people could say, "The Spirit is poured on us from on high, and the desert becomes a fertile field, and the fertile field seems like a forest" (32:15 NIV). The Spirit would return and bring life-giving power along with him!

The prophet Ezekiel went even further. He declared that the renewing power of the Spirit would not just fall on a nation but would land *inside* the hearts of God's people. God promised, "I will put my Spirit within you, and cause you to walk in my statutes and be careful to obey my rules" (Ezekiel 36:27).

Do you hear the intimacy? The very Spirit of God will be *in us*. Do you hear the power? This Spirit will *move us* to obey the decrees of God. When the wind returns, a moral renovation occurs from the inside out. The One who brings the wind will come not to dismiss the law but to give us the internal power and inclination to keep it.

Then, in the powerful imagery of chapter 37, God took Ezekiel to a valley filled with dry bones. The Lord asked Ezekiel if these bones could live. Ezekiel tactfully answered, "O Lord GOD, you know" (v. 3).

God called for Ezekiel to prophesy over the field. Notice the play on words: "[God] said to me, 'Prophesy to the breath; prophesy, son of man, and say to the breath, Thus says the Lord GOD: Come from the four winds, O breath, and breathe on these slain, that they may live.' So I prophesied as he commanded me, and the breath came into them, and they lived and stood on their feet, an exceedingly great army" (vv. 9–10).

Moving to verses 13 and 14: "'Then you will know that I am the LORD, when I have opened your graves and caused you to come up out of your graves, My people. And I will put My Spirit within you and you will come to life, and I will place you on your own land. Then you will know that I, the LORD, have spoken and done it,' declares the LORD" (NASB).

God declared that a day will come when the wind will blow. The breath will come. The Spirit will be placed inside of God's people. And they will come to life.

GOD'S EMPOWERING
PRESENCE WITHIN US

Hundreds of years later, John the Baptist arrived on the scene. He called the nation to repent and prepare for the coming of the Lord. When the people asked him if he was the chosen one they'd been waiting for, John said no. Another was coming.

Listen to how John described him: "I baptize you with water, but he who is mightier than I is coming, the strap of whose sandals I am not worthy to untie. He will baptize you with the Holy Spirit and fire" (Luke 3:16).

I baptize you with water. He will baptize you with the wind!

Days later Jesus inaugurated his earthly ministry by coming to John to be baptized. In that powerful scene, the Father spoke a word of blessing over his Son, and the Holy Spirit descended upon him in bodily form like a dove (v. 22). The boy with the wind was here.

If anyone missed that moment, Jesus said in his first sermon, "The Spirit of the Lord is upon me, because he has anointed me to proclaim good news to the poor. He has sent me to proclaim liberty to the captives and recovering of sight to the blind, to set at liberty those who are oppressed" (4:18).

The Spirit was with him, and he promised to give that same Spirit to God's people!

The Pharisee Nicodemus came to Jesus looking for answers on how to be right with God. Jesus answered, "Unless one is born of water and the Spirit, he cannot enter the kingdom of God" (John 3:5). Then he used a familiar analogy: "The wind blows where it wishes, and you hear its sound, but you do not know where it comes from or where it goes. So it is with everyone who is born of the Spirit" (v. 8).

Nicodemus did not follow the argument. "How can these things be?" he asked.

Jesus answered, "Are you the teacher of Israel and yet you do not understand these things?" (vv. 9–10). How are you missing this, Nick? This is what was lost at the garden! This is what was promised through the prophets!

Jesus did not come just to forgive sins. He came to move sin out of the way so that the intimate, empowering relationship with God could return. Jesus wanted the soul-satisfying and soul-empowering presence of the Spirit to dwell within us.

John told us that Jesus actually shouted this at the top of his lungs. Here's how he described that moment: "On the last day, the great day of the feast, Jesus stood and cried out, saying, 'If anyone is

JESUS CAME SO THAT THE INTIMATE, EMPOWERING RELATIONSHIP WITH GOD COULD RETURN.

thirsty, let him come to Me and drink. The one who believes in Me, as the Scripture said, "From his innermost being will flow rivers of living water." But this He said in reference to the Spirit, whom those who believed in Him were to receive; for the Spirit was not yet given, because Jesus was not yet glorified" (John 7:37–39 NASB).

By "glorified" John meant Jesus' death as our substitute. Sin severed our intimate connection with the Spirit of God. So, to his everlasting praise, Jesus came to deal with sin so the Spirit could return.

On the night of his betrayal, Jesus spoke of this to his disciples: "It is to your advantage that I go away, for if I do not go away, the Helper will not come to you. But if I go, I will send him to you" (John 16:7). He was saying that when he conquered sin and death, then, and only then, would intimacy and life come back. So he needed to go.

And he did go. Our Hero endured the cross. He suffered the severing of intimacy with God. He who knew no sin became sin so that we could be right with God. The sacrifice of his perfect life paid the debt of our sin in full.

If you are imprisoned, how do you know your debt to society is paid? The prison doors are opened. The same is true with our debt of sin, as Tim Keller wrote: "How do we know [Jesus] actually paid the debt in full? Because the door of death opened, and he went out."[5]

Do you know one of the first things John reported about Jesus' reunion with his disciples? He said that Jesus "breathed on them and said to them, 'Receive the Holy Spirit'" (John 20:22). Do you think they understood why he breathed on them? They might have wondered if Jesus had become a little odd after his resurrection.

I have to believe Jesus loved that imagery. "The breath you lost, I brought back. The door is now open for the wind to return. The intimate, animating presence of God can now empower you to live in a whole new way."

Right before he ascended, Jesus told them that when the Spirit came they would receive power so they could be his witnesses. And, according to Acts 2, that is exactly what happened: "Suddenly there came from heaven a sound like a mighty rushing wind, and it filled the entire house where they were sitting. . . . They were all filled with the Holy Spirit and began to speak in other tongues as the Spirit gave them utterance" (vv. 2, 4).

This outpouring of the Spirit was not just for the special few. When a crowd gathered to marvel at this event, Peter explained to them what they were witnessing: "Exalted to the right hand of God, [Jesus] has received from the Father the promised Holy Spirit and has poured out what you now see and hear" (v. 33 NIV). He continued, "Repent, and each of you be baptized in the name of Jesus Christ for the forgiveness of your sins; and you will receive the gift of the Holy Spirit" (v. 38 NASB).

This was the goal: the removal of iniquity for the return of intimacy. The Son buried our sin so we could be alive in the power of the Spirit.

IT'S PART OF BEING IN GOD'S FAMILY

This is an essential aspect of being a Christian. Scripture tells us, "If anyone does not have the Spirit of Christ, they do not belong to Christ" (Romans 8:9 NIV). It is "those who are led by the Spirit of God" who are the children of God (v. 14 NIV). "For we were all baptized by one Spirit so as to form one body . . . we were all given the one Spirit to drink" (1 Corinthians 12:13 NIV).

Paul connected this idea of believers receiving the Spirit with sonship. He said, "God sent forth his Son, born of woman, born under the law, to redeem those who were under the law, so that we might receive adoption as sons. And because you are sons, God has sent the Spirit of his Son into our hearts, crying, 'Abba! Father!'" (Galatians 4:4–6).

Paul told the believers in Ephesus who were not Jews, who had not heard these prophecies or known of their coming, how exactly they could get in on this deal. "In Him, you also, after listening to the message of truth, the gospel of your salvation—having also believed, you were sealed in Him with the Holy Spirit of the promise, who is a first installment of our inheritance, in regard to the redemption of God's own possession, to the praise of His glory" (Ephesians 1:13–14 NASB).

• • •

As we close this chapter, let's make sure we see ourselves in the story.

When you put your faith in Christ, you became God's child and he sent the Spirit of his Son into your heart. When you heard the good news of Jesus and believed it, you were sealed with the promised Holy Spirit. This indwelling of the Spirit is an essential aspect of what it means to become a Christian.

Salvation involves the removal of sin, but that is only a part of it. God's goal was to make a way for us to have communion with him again. As believers we can say, "The love of God has been poured out within our hearts through the Holy Spirit who was given to us" (Romans 5:5 NASB). The intimacy with the Almighty that we long for and the power to fulfill our created intent come with the Spirit's arrival in our hearts.

This is why Paul told the Galatians, "If we live by the Spirit, let us also keep in step with the Spirit" (5:25). None of what we have talked about thus far in this book is possible without the power of the

Spirit of God blowing through our lives. And this raises a very natural question: How does one keep in step with the Spirit? What does his guidance look like? How do we know we're doing it right? Those practical implications of the Spirit alive and working in us, and our choice to cooperate with him—that's what we'll explore in the next chapter.

Now that you've heard the story of the Spirit, just sit for a beat and process the generosity of God. Celebrate that his goal in salvation was to establish *intimacy with you*!

Your Father and your Hero went to the greatest lengths imaginable to give you the powerful presence of the Helper—to change the way you do life. How do you want to respond?

RHYTHMS OF REST

1. What stood out to you in this chapter? Why?
2. How do you feel about the fact that God wants to be as close to you as your own breath? Is this exciting? Comforting? Intimidating? Concerning? Consider writing out how you feel about God's intimate and empowering presence in our lives.
3. Take a moment and write out what questions you have about how exactly "keeping in step with the Spirit" works.

CHAPTER 14

IN STEP WITH THE SPIRIT

In 1914 Sir Ernest Henry Shackleton set sail for the Antarctic with the ambitious goal of leading an expedition across the entire continent. When their ship, *Endurance*, became trapped and then crushed by the ice, their mission became a fight for survival. They were able to make it to a small, inhospitable island, but with desperate cold and shortage of food they would die without rescue. So in a last-ditch effort, a few of the men piled into a tiny lifeboat and attempted an impossible eight-hundred-mile journey to a shipping lane where they might find help.

Straining at the oars through the rough seas, they moved at an agonizingly slow pace, a rate of one mile every half hour or so. At that pace there was no hope for survival. But then, they crossed the 60th parallel of latitude and entered what is known as Drake Passage.

Author Alfred Lansing describes this area of the ocean as the place where "nature has been given a proving ground on which to demonstrate what she can do if left alone."[1] The low atmospheric pressure in the vicinity of the Antarctic Circle draws in high pressure from the north, which creates almost ceaseless, gale-force winds. The US Navy's *Sailing Directions for Antarctica* explains that these westerly winds "are often of hurricane intensity with gust velocities sometimes attaining 150 to 200 miles per hour. Winds of such violence are not known elsewhere, save perhaps within a cyclone."[2]

When Shackleton and his haggard crew rowed their tiny boat into the passage, they hoisted their little sail into the wind—and shot forward as if launched from a cannon. In less than two days, they covered 238 miles of ocean! They reached their destination, a whaling station on the small island of South Georgia, and were able to send boats back to rescue the rest of the expedition.

What was impossible through the strength of their arms, Shackleton and his men accomplished through their skill at harnessing the wind.

If we want the power of the wind of God in our lives, then we must become skilled at accessing it. What does that look like?

When Jesus headed out into the wilderness to be tempted by the devil, he "was *led* up by the Spirit into the wilderness" (Matthew 4:1). Then, when the time of testing was complete, Jesus "returned in the *power* of the Spirit" (Luke 4:14). These two verses provide helpful headings for us when we consider how the Spirit operates in our lives: he *leads* us and he *empowers* us.

THE SPIRIT LEADS US

When Jesus prepared his disciples for the Spirit's arrival, he told them, "I will ask the Father, and he will give you another Helper, to be with you forever" (John 14:16).

In Greek the word translated as "helper" is a combination of the words that mean "walk" and "alongside."[3] Jesus promised to send a counselor who would walk alongside his people.

The word *another* means another of the same kind. He would be like Jesus—except the Spirit would always walk with and live in God's people.

So how do we keep in step with the Spirit? What does his counsel sound like? How do we even know his voice? Let me give you four critical ways the Spirit of God guides us in life.

1. HIS GUIDANCE IS CONSISTENT WITH SCRIPTURE

The Spirit will always be consistent with the Scriptures. As Jesus explained the Spirit's role to the disciples, he told them, "The Helper, the Holy Spirit, whom the Father will send in my name, *he will teach you* all things and bring to your remembrance all that I have said to you" (John 14:26). One of the Spirit's primary roles in the disciples' lives would be to teach them, reminding them of the words of Jesus.

He even referred to the Helper as "the Spirit of truth" and explained, "He will guide you into all the truth, for he will not speak on his own authority, but whatever he hears he will speak, and he will declare to you the things that are to come. He will glorify me, for he will take what is mine and declare it to you. All that the Father has is mine; therefore I said that he will take what is mine and declare it to you" (John 16:13–15).

How do we discern the voice of the Spirit? He will sound like everything you hear Jesus say in the Gospels. The Spirit wants us to know the mind of Christ. The Spirit of God loves the Word of God.

I had a young man approach me at church and ask me how he could learn to hear from God. I told him to read the Scriptures every day until his thoughts instinctually flowed along the channels of the revealed Word of God.

"No, I want to hear from the Spirit," he clarified.

I told him that the apostle Paul called the Scriptures "God-breathed" (2 Timothy 3:16 NIV). This description beautifully encapsulates what Peter explained: "No prophecy of Scripture comes from someone's own interpretation. For no prophecy was ever produced by the will of man, but men spoke from God as they were carried along by the Holy Spirit" (2 Peter 1:20–21). The Spirit of truth breathed out these words through the authors of this book.

This young man was learning that hearing from the Spirit required becoming familiar with the Word.

If you want to hear the Spirit's voice, know his mind, and receive his guidance, then soak your mind with the words he inspired!

Sometimes in church culture there is a tension between "Spirit-led people" and "Bible people." The Spirit does not know that distinction. Again, the Spirit of God loves the Word of God.

This is great news for those who want to know the mind of God. When you sit with the Scriptures, the Holy Spirit of God is far more excited about you understanding them than you are. And when the wind of God blows in your heart as you fill your mind with the thoughts of God—look out. That's where lives change!

Several years ago I read a book entitled *Fire*, which told the harrowing tales of some of the largest forest fires in America's history.[4] While describing the awesome power of these blazes, the author unpacked how a fire can reach such epic proportions. He called it the "fire triangle" because all fires need three elements in order to stay burning: *fuel*, *heat*, and *wind*. If you have those three, then the fire triangle is stable, and the blaze will keep going. Lose one of them, and the fire will go out.

So it is with our fire of passion for God.

It must have the *fuel* of God's Word in our minds. It must have the

IF YOU WANT TO HEAR THE SPIRIT'S VOICE, SOAK YOUR MIND WITH THE WORDS HE INSPIRED.

heat of our affections for God. And it must have the *wind* of the Spirit blowing through our lives. Just reading the Book without the Spirit guiding us could make us arrogant people (1 Corinthians 8:1). That was the problem of the Pharisees in Jesus' day and it's the problem of all legalists today. We need to have a heart that loves the Lord. But if the wind doesn't blow, the fire of our love cannot continue to burn.

The Puritans used to talk about the spiritual life as light for the mind and heat for the heart. We need the Spirit to give us both illumination and affections.

This is why, every time I sit down to read God's Word, I pray that he would open my eyes to discover wonderful things in his law (Psalm 119:18). The wonderful things are there, but I am asking him to open my eyes to see them. Then I ask him to "incline my heart to [his] testimonies, and not to selfish gain" (v. 36).[5]

I need God to move my heart to make these instructions become love. So I ask for the wind to blow into my devotional moment with him. I can build the altar. I can make time to stack up the fuel of his Word in my mind, but I need the wind to blow in order for that fuel to become the fire of affection and action.

How do you know the voice of the Spirit? He will sound like God's Word.

Conversely, he won't sound anything like your flesh.

2. HIS COUNSEL IS CONTRARY TO THE FLESH

Paul told the Galatians, "Walk by the Spirit, and you will not carry out the desire of the flesh. For the desire of the flesh is against the Spirit, and the Spirit against the flesh; for these are in opposition to one another, in order to keep you from doing whatever you want" (Galatians 5:16–17 NASB).

The flesh and the Spirit are at odds. They have totally different agendas, so they won't sound alike. But you may ask, How do I know which is controlling me?

According to Paul it's obvious: "The deeds of the flesh are evident, which are: sexual immorality, impurity, indecent behavior, idolatry, witchcraft, hostilities, strife, jealousy, outbursts of anger, selfish ambition, dissensions, factions, envy, drunkenness, carousing, and things like these, of which I forewarn you, just as I have forewarned you, that those who practice such things will not inherit the kingdom of God" (vv. 19–21 NASB).

Does the voice you sense inside invite you to practice sorcery? That's not the Spirit. Does it prompt you to harshly criticize someone on social media? Not him either. Does it invite you to stew in resentment? He doesn't sound like that. The more we practice the discipline of thinking about what we are thinking about, the easier it will become to discern our thought's source. And we'll be able to confirm we've followed the Spirit's inner prompting when we see the results he produces: "The fruit of the Spirit is love, joy, peace, patience, kindness, goodness, faithfulness, gentleness, self-control; against such things there is no law" (v. 22–23 NASB).

There are many debates about what exactly a manifestation of the Spirit looks like in a person's life. Does he prompt singing? Dancing? Laughter? Crying? Maybe. What we can know for sure is that his presence prompts being loving, patient, faithful, and gentle.

3. HE BUILDS AND PRESERVES COMMUNITY

Here's another telltale sign of the Spirit's work: he is a builder of healthy relationships, not a destroyer.

In his letter to the Ephesians, Paul unflinchingly brought up the hostility that existed between Jews and Gentiles. But in Jesus the division between them had been broken down; he reconciles people not just to God but also to one another. Though we are from different backgrounds ethnically, politically, socially, and spiritually, all of us "through [Jesus] . . . have access in one Spirit to the Father" (Ephesians 2:18). Paul told this community that they were "being built together into a dwelling place for God by the Spirit" (v. 22). The Spirit is about the business of building people together into a living house of worship.

As we discussed earlier, some people today say, "I am spiritual but not religious." Maybe you've said it too. Some people with that mindset have been truly hurt by abusive decisions made by the leadership of different churches. I have known people who've gone through that and always feel a great swell of sympathy and sadness when they tell their stories. If that's your experience, I'm so sorry for what happened to you.

However, I do not think this means that people who have gone through that kind of experience should give up on being a part of a vibrant church community. You don't give up on doctors if you go to a bad one; you find a better one. The same is true of church. Don't quit the institution if you have had a bad experience. Take time to process your wounds. Get counseling and all the help you need to heal. Then pursue reconciliation if possible, or integrate into another church community.

I think many of us, if we are honest, use the "spiritual but not religious" idea as a smoke screen to hide selfishness. We want to say we have a spiritual side, but we don't want the hassle of other people. We do not want the inconvenience of serving. Under the guise of a noble rejection of a broken institution, we buy into a consumerism version of church. *I'll attend if it helps me, but I don't want the hassle of investing in others.* I'm going to challenge whether this can be called "spiritual," because the Spirit loves bringing people together who used to be as far apart as possible.

When Paul addressed this hostility issue with the Ephesians, he had no illusions that making a change would be easy. That's why he implored them to humbly, gently, patiently, and diligently "maintain the unity of the Spirit in the bond of peace" (Ephesians 4:3). It was an active pursuit that would require a specific heart attitude.

The Spirit works to build the church. We work diligently to preserve it.

Paul told the Corinthians that within the church "there are varieties of gifts, but the same Spirit. . . . To each is given the manifestation of the Spirit for the common good" (1 Corinthians 12:4, 7). The Spirit of God has not given anybody *all* his gifts. Rather, he has scattered his gifts among us, so that as we worship, serve, and live together we use these gifts to help one another. Your spiritual gifts are for the group. He equips each of us to build up all of us.

So if you are walking with the Spirit of God, he will lead you to get involved at a local church where you can use the gifts he gave you for the common good. We need you! And you need us!

In Ephesians 5 Paul called believers to "be filled with the Spirit" (v. 18) and then, to explain more, he wrote a massive run-on sentence with five participles. A participle is a verb that participates with the main verb, filling out its meaning. So this passage gives us a good idea of what it looks like to be filled with the Spirit, according to Paul.

It will result in: (1) addressing one another in psalms and hymns and spiritual songs, (2) singing, (3) making melody to the Lord with your heart, (4) giving thanks always and for everything to God the Father in the name of our Lord Jesus Christ, and (5) submitting to one another out of reverence for Christ (Ephesians 5:19–21).

Do you see the community emphasis? The Spirit of God loves the people of God! Where the Spirit leads, encouraging and serving others results.

4. HE EXALTS CHRIST FIRST AND FOREMOST

The final way you can recognize the guidance of the Spirit: he loves to exalt Jesus. Jesus told his disciples in John 16:14, "He will glorify me, for he will take what is mine and declare it to you."

The Spirit desires to shine the spotlight on Jesus. I heard it said once that the Spirit is the shy one in the Trinity. There is truth to it. He is not looking for the spotlight. In fact, he likes to operate the spotlight—and point it right at Jesus!

When the book of Acts records the Spirit moving in power, the name of Jesus is lifted up. Indeed, all throughout Scripture he is called "the Spirit of Christ." So if a "spiritual" movement moves you at all away from the Scriptures and from a focus on the person of Jesus, it is the wrong spirit. The Holy Spirit loves to celebrate Jesus, and he is delighted when you do too.

THE SPIRIT EMPOWERS US

Having the Spirit's guidance is vital, but there's more. We also need his power. We cannot accomplish the call of God on our lives by our willpower alone.

So how do we access the power of the Spirit in our lives?

I used to preach at a lot of camps for middle school students. I loved to call out the question, "Who in here likes fruit?" Dozens of hands would go up. "Who likes apples?" Arms eagerly reached to the sky.

Then I'd call on a little guy to stand up. I'd invite him, "Tell us all, what is your favorite kind of apple?" The best were rural camps where that was actually a hard question for them to answer. *Granny Smith? Golden Delicious? Gala? Gotta decide.* They'd finally commit: "Golden Delicious."

Then I'd ask, "Alright, then tell us, how long does it take you to grow one off your arm?" This question was usually met with confused silence. Sometimes accompanied by glances at peers for support. I'd repeat, "It's not a hard question. About how long does it take you to grow one off your arm?"

Inevitably they'd respond, "I can't."

"What? What was that? You can't grow one? Why not? Do you lack the chlorophyll?" More bewildered stares. Finally I would ask, "So if you want an apple, where do you go to get one?"

The point I was making with those kids was that if you want fruit, you must go to the tree with the power to produce it. The same is true of the fruit of the Spirit. We can't come up with any of his fruit on our own.

I remember growing up hearing many sermon series about Galatians 5:22–23 and the fruit of the Spirit. Each Sunday was dedicated to motivating you to do them. Be loving! Be joyful! Be peaceful! But how do I produce those desires? Have you ever tried to make yourself love someone? How impossible is that?! But then I heard someone ask a simple, mind-blowing question about that passage: "Whose fruit is it?"

The fruit of the Spirit is his to give, not ours to create. He provides what we cannot produce.

Our role is seen in Galatians 5:25: "If we live by the Spirit, let us also keep in step with the Spirit." If we want the manifestations of his presence—love, joy, peace, etc.—then we must walk step by step with him.

"Work out your own salvation with fear and trembling," Paul told believers (Philippians 2:12). The implications of our radical change in identity should manifest in our activity. But Paul also told them, "It is God who works in you, both to will and to work for his good pleasure" (v. 13).

The inclination and the ability to live a spiritual life comes through the power of the Spirit.

COMMAND ME AND GIVE ME
WHAT YOU COMMAND

I love the language of keeping "in step with the Spirit." It paints the picture of moment-by-moment dependence. *Sure, Ben, but what does that picture actually look like?* I'll tell you how it looks in my life. In the morning I sit with the Lord in the secret place, with Scripture and prayer. Then I walk with him through every public space, regularly looking for his wise leading and asking for his powerful help.

For me, this means I constantly pray as Augustine taught people to pray: "Command me, Lord, and give me what you command."[6] If I am to live a supernatural life, I need supernatural resources. In order for me to do what I'm called to do, I must actively reposition my mind to a place of acknowledged dependence. I need him every hour—truly, more than that. I need him every step!

I formed this habit of dependence during my college years when I spent a summer living in the inner city of Denver. A diverse assembly of college students from around the country lived in a church and hosted summer camps in various neighborhoods. At one point we had a camper who was particularly difficult.

She resisted all the rules and disrupted every element of the program. Some of the counselors asked me to try to talk to her, and it did not go well. This young girl had an uncanny ability to insult people. She would instantly identify your insecurities, vocalize them at peak volume, and then mock them endlessly. Usually with a rhythmic cadence. I found the experience humiliating and enraging, even as I marveled at her unique skill. *Why would you say that? And how were you able to make it rhyme?!*

By the fourth day of camp, I was tired. I rose early to have my devotional time with God before the busyness of the day. I tried the usual *Thank you for this day* boilerplate kind of prayer, but I stopped myself. If that kind of prayer was a Christian version of a pump-up speech, I just wasn't having it that day. I decided to get honest.

God, I don't want to go do camp today. I don't love these kids. I don't even like them. I would rather watch TV all day than hang out with them. I would rather stare at a wall than be with these kids! But this is a problem, because the bus is coming. Please help me.

I thought about how I had no love in my heart for that little girl. But I knew God did. So I asked him if he would give some to me. Then I headed off to camp.

It did not take long until she was acting up again, and they sent her to me. She approached me and gave full vent to her anger. High-pitch, high-volume, ferocious anger, leveled at my face. But something was different in me. As I watched her, I didn't feel defensive and angry anymore. I felt profoundly sad.

In a moment the realization hit me: she did not really know me at all. None of this was personal. It's hurt people who hurt people. And this dear child had been hurt.

I saw in my mind's eye a picture of her being happy. Smiling. Playing. Feeling safe. Doing the things little girls are supposed to do at her age. The contrast between that delightful mental image and the distorted reality in front of me broke my heart. I found myself begging God to heal her pain. To bless her. To give her peace. To let her know the peace and joy only he could give. I discovered in my chest a deep and profound love for this child, all while she was still cursing me.

She got kicked out of camp the next day—for fighting, again. This was not a surprise. But what did surprise me was what happened next. As people escorted her to the bus that would take her home, she turned and walked right up to me. She looked straight into my eyes and said, "You were the one who was nice to me."

And that broke my heart. Because I knew the truth. Within my own constitution, I did not possess a reservoir of love for this little girl. But God had an ocean of love for her. He heard a desperate prayer and empowered me to love in a way I could not on my own.

It was then that I realized I wanted to live as many seconds of my life as possible just like I had with this young girl. I wanted to make choices that were fueled by the inexhaustible stream of love, power, courage, wisdom, and integrity that the Spirit of God provides. I wanted to keep in step with him.

I try to whisper prayers of this nature every time a new conversation with someone begins. I started doing this after preaching sermons, when I'd stand out in the lobby and visit with people. Inevitably through the course of a few hours I would receive multiple questions on a variety of subjects. Some theological in nature, but most were requests for wisdom on how to navigate some area of life that was causing acute emotional pain. It required a level of tact and sensitivity that I did not naturally possess. So this habit of quickly and quietly requesting divine assistance kept me humble. If I spouted off advice from the top of my head, that would possess little value. But as I acknowledged God's presence and my dependence, I was better positioned to empathize with a struggling person and access the words of God that have helped me in times past.

True spirituality looks like constant dependence. What or who have you been depending on lately?

God has sent you his Spirit "to help you and be with you forever"

(John 14:16 NIV). Are you paying attention to him? He's right there to guide and empower you.

Soak up Scripture day after day so you can hear his voice and notice his leading. Work out your salvation by opening yourself up to him time and again, inviting the Lord to manifest the fruit of the Spirit in you.

We were made alive by the Spirit; may we walk by the Spirit too.

RHYTHMS OF REST

1. Look back at the ways we discern the Spirit's leadership. Did any of it surprise you?
2. All of us have areas of our lives where we have matured greatly and other areas where we need work. Are there areas right now in which you see the fruit of the Spirit?
3. Pause for a moment to consider what moment-by-moment dependence on the grace of God might look like on a typical day.

CHAPTER 15

TAKE HEART WHEN TROUBLES COME

It was supposed to be a rejuvenating retreat. A time to walk on the beach. Think. Pray. Bask in the beauty of the sunset over the ocean. Most importantly, in that bubble of tranquility I was going to write a book on how to excel at the spiritual life. This book would be formed in the womb of a glorious beach house. What I experienced was quite the opposite.

When I sat down to write, a million competing thoughts came rushing to mind, making it completely impossible to lock on to a single line of thought. As you can imagine, this felt extremely discouraging.

Next, I received a steady barrage of tragic news in a variety of areas: our personal finances, a friend's mental health, a strategic decision we were trying to make as a church, a relationship with eroding trust. It felt as though each day a new boulder of emotional weight was being tossed into a backpack I was forced to carry.

Then I couldn't sleep. I was exhausted after multiple eighteen-plus-hour days of ministry, but when I lay down, I was plagued by lustful thoughts. Incessantly. The voice of lust had chosen that moment to put a full-on rush on the quarterback of my mind, so throughout the night I was wide awake, fighting it off.

My tranquil retreat was not a place of peace at all. I wanted rest. What I got was war.

Why am I confessing all of this to you? These were the opening days of writing the book you now hold in your hands. When I finally sat down to write it, the floodgates of crazy were unleashed on that little beach house.

Life is very hard, and it is not fair. Trials from without and temptations from within threaten to sink us all the time. Some crash on the rocks of moral compromise. Some are torn apart by the waves of opposition. Some slowly sink from taking on the water of disappointment and sadness. These are hard seas to navigate.

I want you to know that even if you implement every word of counsel in the preceding pages, trials and temptations are still coming. And I don't want you to beat yourself up about it. They're coming for all of us. Your struggles are not a sign that you are worse than the rest of us. It's a sign you are one of us.

When you begin to establish a good rhythm in life, something will swerve into your lane and mess up your stride. When you build a beautiful life, something will crash into it and make a mess. Endless frustrations await you when you set this book down and head into the world.

So what do you do?

I think about a popular line a friend of mine says about his recovery program: "It works if you work it."[1] When moments of frustration and temptation rage forward, I like to say to myself, "Excel at the revealed things." God has given us structures and strategies for our spiritual lives, and they work if we work them. So whatever may come our way, let's decide to keep excelling at that which he has revealed.

The writer of Hebrews called us to keep moving forward no matter what: "Let us throw off everything that hinders and the sin that so easily entangles. And let us run with perseverance the race marked out for us" (Hebrews 12:1 NIV).

That passage encapsulates this book so well. We disentangle ourselves from every destructive pattern of thinking or behaving that might encumber us. Then we commit ourselves to run the course that our God has set out for us!

Notice the writer of Hebrews added that we must do all of this "with perseverance." A burst of power can win a battle, but we need endurance if we want to succeed in the war. We need to foster the voice inside of us that says, *I will never stop.*

I know this is easier said than done, because the struggle never ends and the devil doesn't play fair. He'll exploit your weaknesses to seduce you, then turn around and shame you for succumbing to them. He entices and accuses and he doesn't let up. The fight is both personal and persistent.

Paul used the word *wrestle* to describe our spiritual struggles (Ephesians 6:12). When you wrestle someone, your bodies are close. You can feel their breath. Wrestlers grab their opponents and pull them in tight. Temptation is like this. It gets personal. It wraps itself around your insecurities and squeezes you where you are weak. It won't let you tap out. You're going to have to resolve to fight back and continue fighting back every single day of your life.

I know that doesn't sound like super great news. You may be thinking, *Ben, it's the end of the book—send us off with a pump-up speech!*

Let me give you some hope here. Though the fight never ends,

persistent problems do not mean we are destined never to make progress.
I am not calling you to a vain endeavor. Great ground can be covered
if you do not give up.

SUBSTANTIAL HEALING

When Donna and I bought our current home, it had been empty for
almost twenty years. Well, no people had lived there. Animals had
moved in. So had mold. And dust. And water. There were also shelves
upon shelves of porcelain doll heads, bodies, and hair, because the
previous tenant had made porcelain dolls by hand that were in high
demand in the sixties and seventies. Half the square footage of the
home had been converted to a doll factory. And after two decades
on the shelf, the assorted body parts of those dolls had not aged well.
Frankly, they were terrifying.

We wanted our home to be a place of warmth and life and joy,
but first we had to clean house. We filled a dumpster with dolls (they
may have escaped into the woods, I cannot confirm or deny). Then
we filled two more dumpsters with junk. We had to rip out walls and
tear out floors. Revitalization required destruction—out with the old.
Then afterward we were able to repair, replace, and rebuild.

Now, after much effort, we have a beautiful, livable space.

Yet so much remains undone! Major projects still lie ahead for us,
and not just fun stuff; some serious repairs are needed. The challenges
of nature continue to degrade the home. We have to keep cleaning out
the dust, picking up things that fall, washing things that have become
dirty. A home is in constant movement toward chaos unless its resident
keeps up with consistent maintenance. The work never stops.

It is the same with us.

The good news is, though the house still needs constant work and maintenance, it is so much better than it was. If you walked in today you would never know it was once a terrifying den of misfit dolls. The improvements have been substantial.

The same might be said of us.

You may have some temptations now that feel all-consuming, but I promise you, friend, it can get better. Persist in the course we've prescribed and, over time, you'll move from sledgehammers and spackling to dusting and mopping. The work can get easier even if it is never over. While we cannot achieve perfection in this life, we can experience real progress. This is what Francis Schaeffer referred to as "substantial healing."[2] And that is an encouraging thought.

STRUGGLE CAN LEAD TO STRENGTH

Here's some more good news: the more you struggle, the stronger you can become. Resistance builds resilience. When we exercise we put our muscles under crisis so they will be forced to grow stronger to compensate. In school we push ourselves to the edges of our mental limits so our limits can be expanded. *When you continue to fight, you will become a better fighter. When you continue to build, you yourself will be built up.* That is why God doesn't relieve us from some of our struggles; he wants to use them to build strength within us. Character is forged in the crucible of chaos.

Helen Keller said, "[The struggle] makes us strong, patient, helpful men and women. It lets us into the soul of things and teaches us that although the world is full of suffering, it is full also of the overcoming of it!"[3]

The writer of Hebrews gave his audience the perspective they needed to persevere, drawing inspiration from those who had gone before them (Hebrews 11). He was reminding them: We are not the first generation to go through a crisis. We are not the first people God has asked to go through something hard. The world is hemorrhaging with pain, and the Scriptures don't sugarcoat life. From the beginning the world has been a mess and nothing works right. However, Scripture does show us that there is beauty in the midst of the brokenness and real good can happen.

Noah lived in a day of unspeakable evil and faced circumstances no one had ever seen before, but in reverent fear he built that ark and saved his family.

Abraham had to leave everything he knew and set out into unknown and dangerous territory, but he did it to establish a strategic location from which the gospel would go out to every family on the planet.

Moses could have laid up, taken it easy, and lived in comfort in Pharaoh's house, but he saw the injustice done to his people and he associated with them. Yes, it was hard and he almost died a lot, but he saved a nation.

Rahab could have stayed quiet and left things alone, but she risked her life for the sake of the Israelite people.

The writer of Hebrews inspired believers by retelling these stories of those who had gone before.

Others have faced hardship and overcome. You can too.

In fact the Hebrews writer explained that the saints who had gone before them hadn't seen the fullness of God's plan revealed, because "apart from [future generations] they should not be made perfect" (11:40).

Their stories, as significant as they were, were part of a larger story—one that God wanted us to be a part of too!

Those saints were faithful in their time and fulfilled God's purposes for them. Imperfectly, to be sure, with bumps and mistakes all along the way. But they did it. And the same God wants to lead us along as well, if we will allow it. They did not usher in the culmination of God's story, because God was issuing an invitation for the following generations to enter the story. It is our turn.

So let's make the choice today, and each day, to lay aside every weight, cast off the sin that clings so closely, and run with endurance the race that is set before us. Let's remember that the same God who led the saints of old wants to lead us through all of our tragedies and triumphs as well.

How do we run our race? We look to Jesus, our ultimate Hero! We are inspired by the past, but we find motivation by "looking to Jesus, the founder and perfecter of our faith, who for the joy that was set before him endured the cross, despising the shame, and is seated at the right hand of the throne of God" (Hebrews 12:2).

I love that language, "the founder and perfecter of our faith."

He is the Originator. The Founder. The Trailblazer. The Pioneer. The Champion. He picked up the machete and hacked a way through the wilderness. And he's the Finisher. He didn't stop halfway through the valley of the shadow of death. He pushed on through to the other side. He blazed a trail right through death and into life eternal and now beckons us to follow.

"You just fix your eyes on me. I already blazed a trail," he tells us. "You don't have to know all things. You just have to know the One who ordained all things. Trust me. I started this thing and I finished it. I created this world and I will redeem it. Walk with me. I walked through this valley; you can too. Fix your eyes on me. I will lead you. You don't have to have every step figured out. Just keep your eyes locked on me. Take a step. Just look at me. I'll be with you."

"I WALKED THROUGH THIS VALLEY; YOU CAN TOO. FIX YOUR EYES ON ME. I WILL LEAD YOU."

RHYTHMS OF A WELL-FOUGHT LIFE

REST & WAR

AUTHORED BY BEN STUART

BACK TO THE MOUNTAIN

At the beginning of this book I told the story of hiking Longs Peak with my friend Ben. As young, fit, and enthusiastic as we were, we still hit a moment when our internal capacities were insufficient for the challenge. It will be the same for us in our spiritual journeys. The right combination of external drama and internal discouragement will beat down and steal the resolve of the best of us. So we have got to stick with our Hero who wants to walk alongside us every step of the way.

Can I tell you the rest of the story of our misadventures on the mountain?

On the side of Longs Peak, our mountaineer guide began to show us how to breathe properly to accommodate for the lack of oxygen in the atmosphere. We fixed our eyes on him and matched the rhythm of our breathing with his. As we did it, a marvelous change occurred. My headache began to subside. My nausea went away. My limbs felt less like dead weights.

Our guide then said resolutely, "C'mon. Let's go to the top."

As soon as I took my first step, I faltered. My legs felt so wobbly and fragile, unfit for this final challenge. "I don't think I have what it takes to make it," I admitted to him. "I'm sorry."

Then came a moment I have thought about often in my twenty-plus years of life since. He leaned in close and said to me, "Grip the back of my belt. You hold on to me, and Ben will hold on to you. I will stamp out footprints in the snow, and when I step up, I'll pull you up with me. I will lead you to the top of this mountain."

I followed his instruction, and sure enough, when he rose up, his power provided what I needed to take my next step. When he rose, I rose. Within a few short minutes, we stood atop one of the highest points in North America and looked down on clouds.

No matter how spiritually in shape we may feel, we will have moments when we are depleted. The calling of God on our lives is simply too high to ascend by our own efforts. If we are going to live the victorious lives he demands of us, we need his supernatural guidance and power.

If we live by the Spirit, let us also walk by the Spirit. True spirituality looks like constant dependence.

• • •

As Ben and I sat atop Longs Peak with our rescuer, we discovered that this mountain man was actually a missionary. He said something in reference to us about God protecting the ignorant (I don't know, I wasn't really paying attention), but the more we talked the more it became apparent that he was as kind as he was strong.

We were nearing the afternoon hours and it was time to get off the top of the mountain. We picked our way back down, a new spring in our step after conquering what only moments ago had seemed insurmountable. Our new swell of optimism faded quickly, however, when we returned to that long, snowy incline that on the way up had crushed all our youthful energy. I hated that place.

Our missionary hero saw our crestfallen looks and responded, "Oh, c'mon guys, this is the best part!"

What? No. This part almost killed us.

He continued, "You don't climb down this part. You sit down and slide. Put your hands behind you to steer. Let's go!" And with that he plopped down at the beginning of the incline for the briefest of moments before he shot down the slope in a spray of snow.

I didn't exactly have a better option. So I sat down for the briefest of moments, and in a flash, I was gone.

Now, I know that people throughout the ages have had incredible experiences, but I am not sure how many people have ever done something this awesome. Flying down that mountainside was a rush! Our guide had instructed us that if we ever felt out of control we should quickly roll onto our stomachs and throw our elbows into the snow to arrest our descent. I tried it and instantly stopped on a dime. Absolutely amazing!

I spun back around and continued my rapid descent. Ahead I saw our guide quickly stop himself, and with good reason. He had reached the point where we had to traverse across the narrow edge back to the Keyhole. A continued slide would send you careening off the side of the mountain into oblivion below. It was time to stop.

So I flipped around again and deployed my new stopping technique I had mastered seconds before. As I turned and looked upward, I saw the smiling face of my friend Ben as he slid down toward me. I also saw his massive shoe right as it made contact with my face. Ben had not slowed down. That kick sent me somersaulting backward, and in the process my legs tangled up with Ben's.

In a heartbeat we found ourselves both face-first careening down the mountain in an uncontrolled slide, at the worst possible moment.

As we shot toward an uncertain future, my eyes landed on our hero just as he saw us coming toward him. Without flinching he immediately pulled two pickaxes out of his backpack and thrust them into the snow. He wrapped his knees around them to anchor himself, then extended his arms wide. He caught us both, depositing us gently on the ledge leading to the Keyhole.

Unbelievable.

We parted ways shortly after that. As Ben and I raced down the rest of the mountain in the fading light, we couldn't help but say to each other, "Do you think he was an angel? I think he might have been an angel!" He showed up right when we needed him and provided for us perfectly.

No matter how strong you are, you will arrive at a moment when your storehouse of energy is depleted. Even after learning and applying all these principles, you still may slip and fall and careen headfirst toward a cliff. Even then, Jesus will be there—not to condemn you but to catch you. This is our King.

Consider him who endured from sinners such hostility against himself, so that you may not grow weary or fainthearted. Fix your eyes on Jesus. Let hope sustain you all the way home. Remember the words of your Hero: "In this world you will have trouble. But take heart! I have overcome the world" (John 16:33 NIV).

So keep running, friend. You've got this. Because he has got you.

ACKNOWLEDGMENTS

This might be the most intimidating section of this book for me to write! *Rest & War* has been a lifetime in the making; there are so many people to thank and not enough words to adequately express all that is in my heart.

Donna: Thank you for reading this book a thousand times. Thank you for raising our children, loving me so well, caring for our church, creating a home environment where we all flourish, inspiring so many people around us, and being an all-around inspirational human. I love you.

Louie and Shelley: Thank you for the enormous amount of trust you have put in Donna and me. Your bold faith inspires us.

Our Passion City, DC, family: I love battling and building alongside each one of you. I would totally go to this church if I weren't the pastor!

Elizabeth, Jon, Taylor, Brennen, Rachel, Morgan, Jacob, and Matthew: You are all heroes. Thank you for leading our church so well.

Kristin and Bethany: Thank you for joyfully persevering through all the tedium to keep this project on the rails!

Mike D: Through a unique set of circumstances, you spent quality time forging the team here in critical days. Thank you.

Our entire Passion family: I am honored to call you family. I love striving side by side together for the sake of the gospel.

Our team leaders: You were in my mind and heart as I wrote much of this.

Our young church: This is for you.

Matt Chandler, Josh Patterson, and the team at The Village: I wrote the earliest versions of these messages while filling in for Matt in those crazy early days of The Village. Thank you for loving D and me so well in our first year of marriage.

Dr. John Hannah: Thank you for introducing me to the writings of John Owen. My time in your class during seminary changed my life.

Chris Sneller: Thank you for introducing me to so many great Christian thinkers and writers.

My Breakaway family: So much of what is in here was worked out while I was preaching, teaching, and living alongside you amazing Aggies. I am grateful to Gregg Matte, Willie Langston, Jerry Cox, Dr. Stephen McDaniel, Jim Giles, and Timothy Ateek. Your mentorship and friendship are precious and are some of God's greatest gifts to me. Gregg, thank you for being a role model and for setting me up at the beach so I could write this!

Graeme, Mike, and Tommy: Thanks for always checking on me. You strengthen my hands in God.

Ken Werlein and my Faithbridge family: So many of these convictions were forged in me during my time with you. You are my family.

Kyle Idleman: Thanks for the great advice on writing and for the time you spent editing forty-thousand-plus words out of this thing! It became a better book as a result.

Kolb, Mari, Jonathan, and Mandy: I am grateful for you and yours beyond measure. Your adventurous lives inspire me.

Mom: Thank you for raising us to walk with the Lord for a lifetime.

Dad: Thank you for giving me a love for the world our God has made and for showing me what it looks like to maintain lifelong friendships.

Kevin Marks and the Passion Publishing team: Your encouragement kept me going in the hardest parts of writing this! Thank you for believing in me and for your extraordinary patience.

Damon Reiss, Kyle Olund, Carrie Marrs, and everyone at HarperCollins Christian Publishing and W Publishing: Thank you for your belief in this project. Your steady stream of encouragement and your commitment inspires and humbles me!

Leighton and the Passion design team: You guys are a fascinating mix of intimidatingly talented and extraordinarily gracious. Well done.

Lysa Terkeurst and team: Thank you for helping me hone the vision and message at a crucial time in the book development process. You are extremely good at what you do.

The Navy SEAL community: Your devotion inspires me daily.

NOTES

CHAPTER 1: THE SURVIVAL GUIDE

1. Renee D. Goodwin et al., "Trends in Anxiety Among Adults in the United States, 2008–2018: Rapid Increases Among Young Adults," *Journal of Psychiatric Research* 130 (November 2020): 441–46, https://doi.org/10.1016/j.jpsychires.2020.08.014.

2. Anjel Vahratian et al., "Symptoms of Anxiety or Depressive Disorder and Use of Mental Health Care Among Adults During the COVID-19 Pandemic—United States, August 2020–February 2021," *Morbidity and Mortality Weekly Report* 70, no. 13 (April 2021): 490–94, https://dx.doi.org/10.15585/mmwr.mm7013e2.

3. Jean M. Twenge, "Have Smartphones Destroyed a Generation?," *The Atlantic*, September 2017, https://www.theatlantic.com/magazine/archive/2017/09/has-the-smartphone-destroyed-a-generation/534198/.

4. Matt Gonzales, "America Is Lonely: The Epidemic Few Are Talking About," The Recovery Village, January 5, 2021, https://www.therecoveryvillage.com/mental-health/news/america-is-lonely/.

5. Justin McCarthy, "Happiness Not Quite as Widespread as Usual in the US," Gallup, January 10, 2020, https://news.gallup.com/poll/276503/happiness-not-quite-widespread-usual.aspx.

6. Branwen Jeffreys, "Do Children in Two-Parent Families Do Better?," BBC News, February 5, 2019, https://www.bbc.com/news/education-47057787.

CHAPTER 2: THE CONQUERING KING

1. C. S. Lewis, *Mere Christianity* (1952; repr., New York: HarperCollins, 1980), 45.
2. This is my very brief summary of ideas presented in Cornelius Plantinga Jr., *Not the Way It's Supposed to Be: A Breviary of Sin* (Grand Rapids, MI: Eerdmans, 1996).
3. Aleksandr Solzhenitsyn, *The Gulag Archipelago: 1918–1956* (New York: Harper & Row, 1974), 168.
4. Inspired by a sermon by John Piper. "The Son of God Appeared to Destroy the Works of the Devil," Desiring God, December 23, 1984, https://www.desiringgod.org/messages/the-son-of-god-appeared-to -destroy-the-works-of-the-devil.
5. Lewis, *Mere Christianity*, 45.

CHAPTER 4: UNDERSTAND THE ENEMY'S PLAYBOOK

1. William Gurnall, *The Christian in Complete Armour: Daily Readings in Spiritual Warfare* (1655, 1658, and 1162; repr., Chicago, IL: Moody Publishers, 1994).
2. *Patton*, directed by Franklin J. Schaffner, starring George C. Scott (Los Angeles: Twentieth Century Fox, 1970).
3. "Who We Are," Center for Humane Technology, accessed October 4, 2021, https://www.humanetech.com/who-we-are#our-story.
4. Tristan Harris, "How a Handful of Tech Companies Control Billions of Minds Every Day," TED, April 2017, https://www.ted.com/talks /tristan_harris_how_a_handful_of_tech_companies_control_billions _of_minds_every_day/transcript.
5. John Owen, *Of Temptation: The Nature and Power of It [. . .]*, in *The Works of John Owen, D.D.*, ed. Rev. William H. Goold (New York: Robert Carter & Brothers, 1852), 132–33.
6. Sun Tzu, *The Art of War*, trans. Leonel Giles (Mineola, NY: Ixia Press, 2019), 40.
7. Paraphrase of Aragorn's words: "Open war is upon you, whether you would risk it or not." *The Lord of the Rings: The Two Towers*, directed by Peter Jackson, starring Viggo Mortensen (Burbank, CA: New Line

Cinema, 2002), quoted in "Open War Is Upon You," published by Dave Cole, January 26, 2013, YouTube video, 00:50, https://www.youtube.com/watch?v=vK0_Ob9qCI0.

CHAPTER 5: ELIMINATE EXPOSURE

1. Jonathan Eig, "Floyd Mayweather Jr.: A Master at Not Getting Hit," *Wall Street Journal*, August 25, 2017, https://www.wsj.com/articles/floyd-mayweather-jr-a-master-at-not-getting-hit-1503657577.

2. Paul Bryant quoted in Domonique Foxworth, "It's Time We Modify Old Adage 'Defense Wins Championships,'" The Undefeated, December 8, 2018, https://theundefeated.com/features/its-time-we-modify-old-adage-defense-wins-championships/.

3. Jeremy Wiles, "15 Mind-Blowing Statistics About Pornography and the Church," Conquer Series, modified August 23, 2021, https://conquerseries.com/15-mind-blowing-statistics-about-pornography-and-the-church.

4. Quoted in James Clear, "This Simple Equation Reveals How Habits Shape Your Health, Happiness, and Wealth," James Clear (website), accessed October 2, 2021, https://jamesclear.com/lewins-equation.

5. Sun Tzu, *The Art of War*, trans. Leonel Giles (Mineola, NY: Ixia Press, 2019), 61.

6. Tzu, *Art of War*, 61.

7. Sun Tzu, "Chapter 9: The Army on the March," SunTzuSaid.com, accessed October 2, 2021, https://suntzusaid.com/book/9.

8. James Clear, *Atomic Habits: An Easy & Proven Way to Build Good Habits & Break Bad Ones* (New York: Penguin Random House, 2018).

9. Rebecca Moody, "Screen Time Statistics: Average Screen Time in US vs. the Rest of the World," Comparitech, June 8, 2021, https://www.comparitech.com/tv-streaming/screen-time-statistics/.

10. Jonathan Edwards, *The Works of Jonathan Edwards*, vol. 1, *Freedom of the Will* (Edinburgh, Scotland: 1834), 23.

11. "What Is Jiu-Jitsu?," Essential Jiu-Jitsu, accessed October 2, 2021, https://www.essentialbjj.com/about-us/what-is-jiu-jitsu/.

12. Georges St-Pierre, "Georges St-Pierre Breaks Down MMA Scenes

from Movies," published by GQ Sports, April 6, 2021, YouTube video, 19:30, https://www.youtube.com/watch?v=cW0WwNZioCo.

13. John Owen, *Overcoming Sin and Temptation,* ed. Kelly M. Kapic and Justin Taylor (Wheaton, IL: Crossway Books, 2006), 205.

14. John Owen, *The Works of John Owen,* ed. William H. Goold and William H. Gross, vol. 6, *Mortification of Sin in Believers* (1854; repr., London: Johnstone and Hunter, 2015), 23–24.

15. "Mayweather Defense | Shoulder Roll | Boxing Technique Breakdown | Film Study," published by Complex Boxing, October 8, 2020, YouTube video, 3:39, https://www.youtube.com/watch?v=2AnWJAz_-9k.

16. Simon Dodson, "Floyd Mayweather, the Greatest Boxer Ever," Medium, November 23, 2019, https://medium.com/@simondodson.com/floyd-mayweather-the-greatest-boxer-ever-9f9e0628591e.

CHAPTER 6: PADDLE DOWNSTREAM

1. Douglas J. Moo, *The Letter of James* (Grand Rapids, MI: Eerdmans, 2000), 76.

2. Johnny Cash, *Cash: The Autobiography* (New York: HarperCollins, 1997), 141.

3. Cash, *Cash,* 141.

4. Grant Hilary Brenner, "Pornography and Broken Relationships," *Psychology Today,* July 17, 2017, https://www.psychologytoday.com/us/blog/experimentations/201707/pornography-and-broken-relationships.

CHAPTER 7: LOOK UPSTREAM

1. Allison Seale, "Arsenic and Old Lakes," AllisonSeale.com, accessed October 2, 2021, http://allisonseale.com/arsenic.html; "Atochem Suffers Arsenic Legacy," ICIS, January 23, 1995, https://www.icis.com/explore/resources/news/1995/01/23/20068/atochem-suffers-arsenic-legacy/; Chris Garlock, "An Environmental Warrior Gone Wrong," *Texas Observer,* January 22, 1999, https://www.texasobserver.org/935-afterword-an-environmental-warrior-gone/; Rachel Knight, "The Rehabilitation of Bryan Municipal Lake: From Past Anxiety

to Future Analysis," *Insite Brazos Valley Magazine*, February 2, 2018, https://insitebrazosvalley.com/the-rehabilitation-of-bryan-municipal -lake-from-past-anxiety-to-future-analysis/.

2. John Owen, *The Works of John Owen, D.D.*, ed. William H. Goold, vol. 6, *Of the Mortification of Sin in Believers, Etc.*, (Edinburgh, Scotland: T & T Clark, 1862), 118.

3. Patrick Carnes, *Out of the Shadows: Understanding Sexual Addiction*, 3rd ed. (Center City, MN: Hazelden, 2001).

4. Owen, *Works of John Owen*, 179.

5. A paragraph from Thomas Chalmers's sermon "The Expulsive Power of New Affection," summarized in Tim Keller, *Counterfeit Gods: The Empty Promises of Money, Sex, and Power, and the Only Hope That Matters* (New York: Penguin Random House, 2009), 186.

6. William Shakespeare, *Romeo and Juliet*, ed. Barbara Mowat and Paul Werstine, Folger Shakespeare Library (New York: Simon & Schuster, 2011), 1.2.99–100, https://shakespeare.folger.edu/shakespeares-works /romeo-and-juliet/.

7. Shakespeare, *Romeo and Juliet*, 2.2.2–6.

8. Saint Augustine, *Confessions*, book 9, chap. 1, available at Christian Classics Ethereal Library, accessed October 3, 2021, https://ccel.org /ccel/augustine/confess/confess.x.i.html#x.i-p0.2.

CHAPTER 8: THE PROPER PURSUIT

1. Jonathan Edwards, *The Works of Jonathan Edwards*, ed. Edward Hickman, vol. 1, *Freedom of the Will* (Edinburgh, Scotland: Banner of Truth, 1979), 237.

CHAPTER 9: FROM ANXIETY TO INTIMACY

1. William Mitchell Ramsay, *The Cities and Bishoprics of Phrygia: Being an Essay of the Local History of Phrygia from the Earliest Times to the Turkish Conquest*, book 6, part 2 (London: Clarendon Press, 1897), 565. Also see Matthew 6:34.

2. William J. Federer, *America's God and Country: Encyclopedia of Quotations* (St. Louis, MO: Amerisearch, 1994), 385.

3. Jeremiah Burroughs, *The Rare Jewel of Christian Contentment* (London, 1651), 49.

4. *Black Hawk Down*, directed and produced by Ridley Scott, starring Josh Harnett and Eric Bana (Los Angeles: Columbia Pictures, 2001).

5. Jeff Struecker, "Bullet Proof Faith," BeliefNet, accessed October 4, 2021, https://www.beliefnet.com/love-family/galleries/bullet-proof -faith.aspx.

6. Patrick Johnstone, *Operation World* (Grand Rapids, MI: Zondervan, 1993).

7. John G. Paton, *John G. Paton: Missionary to the New Hebrides* (1889; repr., Edinburgh, Scotland: Banner of Truth Trust, 1965), 200.

CHAPTER 10: PRODUCTIVE SCHEDULE

1. Viktor Frankl, *The Unheard Cry for Meaning: Psychotherapy and Humanism* (New York: Washington Square Press, 1984), 21.

2. Friedrich Nietzsche, *Twilight of the Idols: Or How to Philosophize with a Hammer*, quoted in Viktor Frankl, *Man's Search for Meaning*, trans. Ilse Lasch (1959; repr., London: Random House, 2004), 109.

3. David T. Tsumura, "The Earth and the Waters in Genesis 1 and 2: A Linguistic Investigation," *JSOT Sup* 83 (1989): 201.

4. John C. Maxwell, *Developing the Leader Within You* (Nashville, TN: Thomas Nelson, 1993), 31.

5. Elisabeth Elliot, *Let Me Be a Woman* (Wheaton, IL: Tyndale, 1999), 17.

CHAPTER 11: PROTECTIVE SAINTS

1. *Navy SEALs: BUDS Class 234*, aired on October 19, 2000, on the Discovery Channel, https://press.discovery.com/emea/dsc/programs /navy-seals-class-234/.

2. Steven Pressfield, *Gates of Fire* (New York: Random House, 1998).

3. Pressfield, *Gates of Fire*, 39.

4. Natalie Baker, "We're Only As Sick As Our Secrets," American Addiction Centers, January 30, 2017, https://www.recovery.org/were -only-as-sick-as-our-secrets/.

CHAPTER 12: POSITIVE RELEASE

1. Phrasing made popular by trauma expert Bessel van der Kolk's bestseller. Bessel A. van der Kolk, *The Body Keeps the Score: Brain, Mind, and Body in the Healing of Trauma* (New York: Penguin, 2014).
2. *The Shorter Catechism of the Westminster Assembly of Divines* (1647; repr., London: Presbyterian Church of England, 1897), 2, https://www.google.com/books/edition/The_Shorter_Catechism_of_the_Westminster/HNxLAAAAMAAJ?gbpv=1.
3. John Piper, *The Roots of Endurance: Invincible Perseverance in the Lives of John Newton, Charles Simeon, and William Wilberforce* (Wheaton, IL: Crossway, 2002), 149.
4. Roland H. Bainton, *Here I Stand: A Life of Martin Luther* (Nashville, TN: Abingdon Press, 1978), 377.
5. Charles H. Spurgeon, *Lectures to My Students: A Selection from the Addresses Delivered to the Students of The Pastor's College, Metropolitan Tabernacle* (London, 1875), 175, google.com/books/edition/Lectures_to_my_students/SXtP6DSz_fUC?hl=&gbpv=1.
6. Spurgeon, *Lectures to My Students*, 172.
7. Jonathan Edwards, *The Works of Jonathan Edwards*, vol. 1 (1834; repr., London: Banner of Truth Trust, 1974), 20, https://www.ccel.org/ccel/edwards/works1/Page_xx.html.

CHAPTER 13: THE STORY OF THE SPIRIT

1. Michael Lipka and Claire Gecewicz, "More Americans Now Say They're Spiritual but Not Religious," Pew Research Center, September 6, 2017, https://www.pewresearch.org/fact-tank/2017/09/06/more-americans-now-say-theyre-spiritual-but-not-religious/.
2. "Spirituality," *Psychology Today*, accessed October 3, 2021, https://www.psychologytoday.com/us/basics/spirituality.
3. Strong's Hebrew Concordance, s.v. "7307. ruach," Bible Hub, accessed October 4, 2021, https://biblehub.com/hebrew/7307.htm.
4. Thomas Wolfe, "God's Lonely Man," in *The Hills Beyond* (New York: New American Library, 1982), 146.

5. Timothy Keller, *Hope in Times of Fear: The Resurrection and the Meaning of Easter* (New York: Penguin Random House, 2021), 32.

CHAPTER 14: IN STEP WITH THE SPIRIT

1. Alfred Lansing, *Endurance: Shackleton's Incredible Voyage* (1959; repr., New York: Basic Books, 2014), 284.
2. *Sailing Directions for Antarctica: Including the Off-Lying Islands South of Latitude 60°* (Washington, DC: US Navy, 1943), 35, https://www.google.com/books/edition/Sailing_Directions_for_Antarctica/gooNAQAAIAAJ?hl.
3. Strong's Greek Concordance, s.v. "3875. paraklétos," Bible Hub, accessed October 4, 2021, https://biblehub.com/greek/3875.htm.
4. Stephen J. Pyne, *Fire: A Brief History* (Seattle, WA: University of Washington Press, 2001), xv.
5. I am indebted to John Piper for this encouragement.
6. Modernized from, "Give what thou commandest and command what thou wilt," in Saint Augustine, *Confessions*, ed. and trans. Albert C. Outler (Dallas: self-pub., 1955), 9, https://www.ling.upenn.edu/courses/hum100/augustinconf.pdf.

CHAPTER 15: TAKE HEART WHEN TROUBLES COME

1. This phrase is chanted as a group at the end of every Alcoholics Anonymous meeting. A. J. Adams, *Undrunk: A Skeptic's Guide to AA* (Center City, MN: Hazelden Publishing), 2009.
2. John Murdock, "Recalling Francis Schaeffer's Christian Environmentalism," First Things, February 22, 2013, https://www.firstthings.com/web-exclusives/2013/02/recalling-francis-schaeffers-christian-environmentalism.
3. Helen Keller, *The World I Live In & Optimism: A Collection of Essays* (Mineola, NY: Dover Publications, 2009), 89.

ABOUT THE AUTHOR

Ben Stuart is the pastor of Passion City Church, Washington, DC. He previously served as the executive director of Breakaway Ministries, a weekly Bible study attended by thousands of college students on the campus of Texas A&M, for eleven years. Ben earned a master's degree in historical theology from Dallas Theological Seminary and is the author of the bestselling *Single, Dating, Engaged, Married: Navigating Life and Love in the Modern Age* and the Bible study *This Changes Everything.* He and his wife, Donna, live to inspire and equip people to walk with God for a lifetime. They reside in the Washington, DC, area with their three kids, Hannah, Sparrow, and Owen.

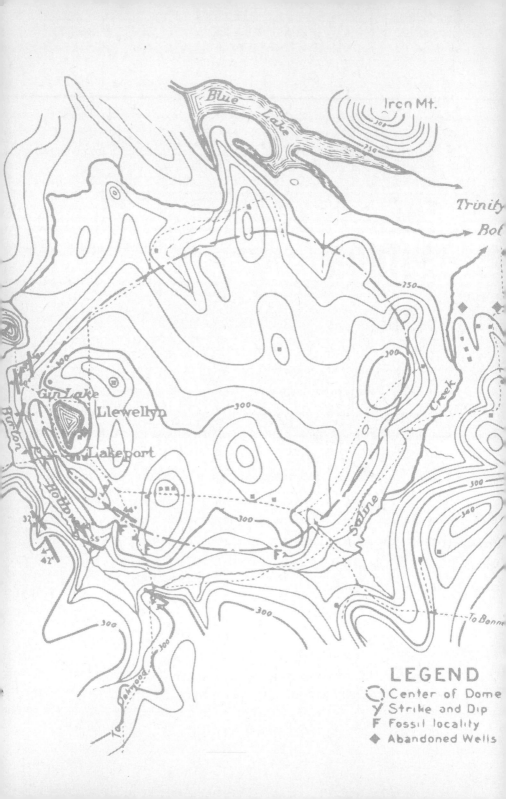

LEGEND
◯ Center of Dome
Y Strike and Dip
F Fossil locality
◆ Abandoned Wells